100 Award-Winning Science Fair Projects

Glen Vecchione

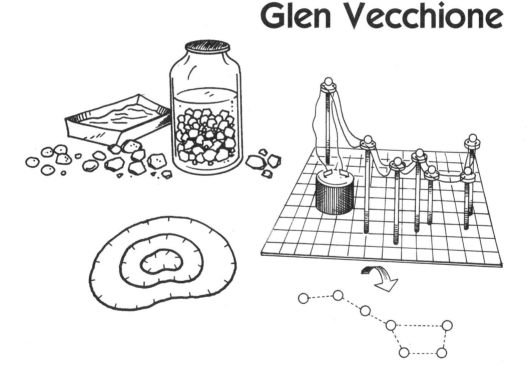

Sterling Publishing Co., Inc.
New York

For Briana and Nicholas

Illustrated by Glen Vecchione
Edited and layout designed by Jeanette Green

Library of Congress Cataloging-in-Publication Data

Vecchione, Glen.
   100 award-winning science fair projects / Glen Vecchione.
      p. cm.
   Includes index.
   ISBN 0-8069-4261-4
   1. Science projects--Juvenile literature. [1. Science projects.
2. Experiments.] I. Title:
   One hundred award-winning science fair projects. II. Title.
   Q182.3 .V428 2001
   507'.8--dc21   2001020189

3 5 7 9 10 8 6 4 2

First paperback edition published in 2002 by
Sterling Publishing Company, Inc.
387 Park Avenue South, New York, N.Y. 10016
© 2001 by Glen Vecchione
Distributed in Canada by Sterling Publishing Co., Inc.
c/o Canadian Manda Group, One Atlantic Avenue, Suite 105
Toronto, Ontario, Canada M6K 3E7
Distributed in Great Britain and Europe by Chris Lloyd at Orca Book
Services, Stanley House, Fleets Lane, Poole BH15 3AJ, England.
Distributed in Australia by Capricorn Link (Australia) Pty. Ltd.
P.O. Box 704, Windsor, NSW 2756 Australia
Printed in China
All rights reserved
Sterling ISBN 0-8069-4261-4 Hardcover
1-4027-0301-5 Paperback

CONTENTS

Metric Equivalents

We've rounded off metric equivalents in these projects for convenience. And most measurements in this book, whether dry or liquid, assume capacity (liquid) measures in convenient milliliter conversions from teaspoons, tablespoons, and cups, etc. (Weights of these dry or liquid substances of course will vary.)

Capacity (Liquid & Dry Measures)

1 minim = $\frac{1}{60}$ fluid dram = 0.00376 cubic inch = 0.06161 milliliter

1 fluid dram = 60 minims = 0.226 cubic inch = 3.697 milliliters

1 milliliter = 0.2 teaspoon = 0.07 tablespoon = 0.034 fluid ounce = 0.004 cup

1 teaspoon = 100 drops = 5 milliliters = $\frac{1}{3}$ tablespoon

1 tablespoon = 3 teaspoons = ½ fluid ounce = 15 milliliters

1 fluid ounce = 2 tablespoons = 30 milliliters = 0.03 liter

1 gill = 4 fluid ounces = 7.22 cubic inches = 118.29 milliliters

1 cup = 16 tablespoons = 8 fluid ounces = 240 milliliters = 0.24 liter

1 pint = 2 cups = 480 milliliters = 0.47 liter

1 quart = 4 cups = 2 pints = 32 fluid ounces = 960 milliliters = 0.95 liter = 57.75 cubic inches

1 liter = 1,000 milliliters = 61.02 cubic inches = 34 fluid ounces = 4.2 cups = 2.1 pints = 1.06 quart (liquid) = 0.908 quart (dry) = 0.26 gallon

1 gallon = 4 quarts = 128 fluid ounces = 3.8 liters = 231 cubic inches

U.S. Dry Measure

1 pint = ½ quart = 33.6 cubic inches = 0.55 liter

1 quart = 2 pints = 67.2 cubic inches = 1.01 liters

Weight (Avoirdupois)

1 gram = 0.035 ounce = 1,000 milligrams = 0.002 pound

1 ounce = 28 grams = 437.5 grains = 0.06 pound

100 grams = 3½ ounces

1 pound = 16 ounces = 454 grams = 0.45 kilogram = 7,000 grains

1 kilogram = 2.2 pounds = 1,000 grams

1 ton = 2,000 pounds = 0.9 metric ton

1 metric ton = 1,000 kilograms = 1.1 tons

Weight (Apothecaries')

1 grain = 0.05 scruple = 0.002083 ounce = 0.0166 dram = 0.0648 gram

1 scruple = 20 grains = 0.333 dram = 1.29 grams

1 dram = 3 scruples = 60 grains = 3.88 grams

1 ounce = 8 drams = 480 grains = 0.083 pound

1 pound = 12 ounces = 5760 grains = 0.37 kilogram

Distance

1 millimeter = 0.039 inch

1 inch = 25 millimeters = 2.54 centimeters = 0.025 meter

1 foot = 12 inches = 30 centimeters = 0.3 meter

1 yard = 3 feet = 36 inches = 90 centimeters = 0.9 meter

1 meter = 100 centimeters = 39.37 inches = 3.28 feet = 1.09 yards (1 yard + $32/5$ inches) = 0.2 rods

1 rod = 5 meters = 16½ feet

1 kilometer = 1,000 meters = 0.6 mile

1 mile = 1,609.3 meters = 1.6 kilometers

Area

1 square centimeter = 0.15 square inch

1 square inch = 6.45 square centimeters

1 square foot = 0.09 square meter

1 square yard = 0.83 square meter

1 square meter = 10.76 square feet = 1.19 square yards

1 acre = 160 square rods = 0.4 hectare = 4,047 square meters

1 hectare = 2.47 acres

1 square kilometer = 0.38 square mile

1 square mile = 2.58 square kilometers

Volume

1 cubic centimeter = 1,000 cubic millimeters = 0.06 cubic inch

1 cubic inch = 16.38 cubic centimeters

1 cubic foot = 1,728 cubic inches = 0.028 cubic meter = 0.037 cubic yard

1 cubic yard = 27 cubic meter = 0.76 cubic meter

1 cubic meter = 1,000,000 cubic centimeters = 35.31 cubic feet= 1.3 cubic yards

Temperature

To convert Centigrade (Celsius) to Fahrenheit degrees, use this formula: $\frac{9}{5}$ °C + 32 = °F

To convert Fahrenheit to Centigrade (Celsius) degrees, use this formula: $\frac{5}{9}$ (°F − 32) = °C

Introduction

Careful Observation & Engagement

Use this book as a starting point for your own scientific explorations. Each of the 100 projects here is designed to introduce new ideas, help you understand new concepts, and raise new questions in your mind. Each project will teach you step-by-step, how to perform an experiment, demonstrate a procedure, or construct a working model that's guaranteed to stand out in a science-fair competition. And every project is spectacular.

Today regional science-fair competitions require participants to research, question, hypothesize, test, and draw conclusions about a timely, controversial, or compelling scientific topic. This procedure follows the scientific method and can be an important factor when judges determine prizewinners. You can better understand the scientific method if you reduce it to five steps.

Scientific Method

1 Research a particular topic.

2 Ask a question related to the topic.

3 Formulate a hypothesis that answers your question.

4 Create an experiment that will prove or disprove your hypothesis.

5 Draw a conclusion from the result of your experiment.

A serious commitment to the scientific method—both in the creation of a project and as a standard for judging projects—presents a dilemma for any author of a science-fair project collection. After all, the true

method requires a grassroots approach to doing all the work, and any book providing "canned" information would contaminate the student's own discovery. Knowing this, we can still say that there are two conditions often overlooked in the successful quest for scientific understanding: observation and engagement.

With these conditions in mind, we've assembled this collection of projects. We feel that the best way to create enthusiasm for compelling scientific topics is through compelling demonstrations. After all, it was the twitch of severed frog's legs that prompted Alessandro Volta to theorize about electricity. It was the whirl of Hero's boiler that inspired the ancient Greeks to experiment further with hydraulic pressure.

In the same spirit, we present make-it-yourself projects that promise to puzzle, engage, and inspire. Assembling or performing them will help you discover their secrets; understanding these secrets will help you appreciate the significance of a project in its broader scientific context. And while engaged in this larger pool, you can perhaps "work backwards" and invent some similar projects of your own.

Over 100 projects have been organized to help you find the topic that most interests you. Although you'll find many projects that require model construction, other projects require collecting data and emphasize analyzing and displaying results attractively. This means that we've included something for everyone—from extracting DNA from chicken livers to collecting depth-sounding data for topographic graphing. And other projects, like "Race for the Epicenter," even require a little game-playing activity by participants. It all adds up to fun, and having fun with science is a great way to learn about science.

Supplies

All projects are safe, and all use inexpensive and easily found materials. Check hardware stores and art, craft, music, medical, chemical, or science supply stores. When appropriate, we suggest alternate materials for project variations. All projects have been built, tested, and redesigned when appropriate to make their result more pronounced or dramatic.

Measurements

Many project measurements have equivalent metric measurements that have been rounded off for convenience. So, to simplify things, we'll say 450 grams or even 500 grams to make a project that requires 1 pound of material, fully aware that the precise metric equivalent of 1 pound is 454 grams. Most measurements in this book, whether dry or liquid, assume capacity (liquid) measures in convenient milliliter conversions from tea-spoons, tablespoons, or cups. Weights of these dry or liquid substances measured in teaspoons, cups, quarts, etc., of course, will vary.

Since hardware and lumber are rarely found in American equivalents abroad, use the standard sizes found in hardware and lumber stores in your country.

To keep you going and to ensure that finding equivalents is a quick and painless process, we include a Metric Equivalents table on page 4.

Experiment, Experiment

Of course, the ultimate goal of a book like ours is to encourage you to do a little experimenting on your own. Redesign a project and share your thoughts with teachers and friends. We hope you do great things in your competition—at whatever level you participate—and that you collect prizes. We know you'll have fun, and we wish you spectacular luck!

Chemists & Cooks

Medieval Paint Palette

You Will Need

- Watercolor mixing tray
- 5 raw eggs
- Mortar and pestle
- Candle
- Narrow paintbrush
- Mister (water-misting bottle)
- Pencil
- 2 small plastic bags
- Hammer
- 2 small screw-top jars
- 5 sheets paper
- Pad vellum paper
- Teaspoon or 5-ml spoon
- Cotton swabs
- Craft knife
- Saucepan
- Teacup and saucer
- For pigments: copper strip (angle irons or hinges), vinegar, lampblack (soot), white chalk, blue aquarium gravel, heliotrope seeds, dried mustard or safflower, tea bag, iron filings, steel wool

This project uses safe materials to recreate the palette of a medieval artist. You will first extract pigments from some of the materials a medieval artist might have used, and then combine, or mull, the pigments with the medium of raw egg yolk.

Medieval artists and book illuminators were practical chemists who often used toxic ingredients to produce brilliant colors. Although many of these ingredients were dangerous or difficult to find—arsenic for yellow, lapis lazuli for blue (safe), mercuric sulfide for red—they were sought after and hoarded, and the most successful recipes for mixing colors were jealously guarded.

Since oil color was unknown until the early 18th century, painters struggled to find a medium that suspended their pigments evenly, allowed them to adhere to various surfaces, and preserved the trueness of their colors. They found their solution in both the yolk and white of a raw egg, and egg tempera became the prevailing method of painting for nearly 800 years.

Preparing the Pigments

Green (Verdigris): Rub the copper strip with steel wool until it begins to shine. Place the strip in a saucer and brush both sides with vinegar. Allow the vinegar to dry and then recoat the strip. Allow this second coat to dry and then mist the strip with a little water. In about 24 hours, a greenish crust will develop on the surface of the copper. When the crust hardens, use the craft  knife to carefully scrape about 1 teaspoon of (5 ml) verdigris from the surface of the copper onto the paper. Then fold and store the paper until you are ready to use the pigment.

Yellow (Safflower Ochre): Mix ½ teaspoon (2.5 ml) of powdered safflower with ½ teaspoon (2.5 ml) of powdered mustard. Fold and store the pigment in paper.

Blue (Lapis Lazuli): Place 1 teaspoon of blue aquarium gravel in a double plastic bag. On a firm, unbreakable surface, tap the hammer across the gravel until you pulverize it into a fine powder. Fold and store the powder in paper.

Red (Turnsole): Remove 1 teaspoon of seeds from the heliotrope (turnsole) vine. Crush the seeds in a mortar with a pestle; then place the crushed seeds in a saucepan with just enough water to cover them. Bring the water to a boil and then allow the seeds to steep. This forms an infusion of seed pigment that will be red, blue, or purple depending on the ripeness of the seeds. Save the infusion in a small screw-top jar. If heliotrope is difficult to find, you can substitute 1 teaspoon of dry paprika.

Black (Lampblack): Hold a lit candle against the smooth side of a saucer until soot accumulates. Carefully brush this soot into a piece of folded paper for storing.

White (Alum White): Grind a piece of white chalk against sandpaper until you have a fine power. Fold and store the powder in paper.

Brown Ink (Sepia Wash): Place the tea bag in a saucepan, and fill the pan with just enough water to cover the tea bag. When the water boils, add ½ teaspoon of iron filings and 3 drops of vinegar. Remove the saucepan from the heat, and allow the mixture to steep overnight. Place the mixture in a small glass jar and screw on the top.

Preparing the Drawing

1. Enlarge the illustration from page 6 or 7 on a photocopy machine. Place a sheet of vellum paper over the enlargement and trace the drawing onto the vellum, using the pencil.

2. Dip the brush in the sepia ink and go over the outline. Leave the line details in the picture's interior for later. Rinse out the brush and allow the ink to dry.

Mixing & Applying the Medium

1. In a teacup, separate the yolks from 5 eggs. Stir the yolks gently and don't allow them to become foamy. Add about ½ teaspoon of yolk to each of the cups in the mixing tray. Fill one of the remaining cups with the sepia ink.

2. Carefully unfold the papers containing your dry pigments, and tap a little pigment into each of the cups, mixing the pigment into the egg yolk with a cotton swab. Add more color to deepen the color; add more white to lighten the color.

3. Brush color onto each of the drawings you copied. In true medieval fashion, start with a light coating of color, allow it to harden, and then apply another coat. For a thicker, more reflective color, apply a coating of white to the surface before applying a color. Dip the brush in water to rinse it before applying another color.

4. After the paint dries, finish your artwork by dipping the brush into the sepia ink again and adding shadows and details to the colors.

Result

With care and patience, your painting will have colors, hues, and shadings very much like those available to medieval painters and manuscript illuminators.

Chemical Properties of Egg Tempera

Egg tempera is the suspension of pigment particles in the medium of the egg yolk. The water of the egg yolk adds viscosity to the pigment, and the fat attaches the pigment to the paper where it can harden. This means that each pigment particle is surrounded by compacted layers of sticky fat.

But eggs are mostly water, and because egg tempera is water-based, it's more transparent than opaque and should be applied thinly, in layers. This is why you use vellum paper, which has a very smooth surface and imitates the smooth parchment that was used at the time. The interesting quality of egg yolk is that the yellow color doesn't detract from the color of the pigments. In fact, with time, the yellowness of the yolk becomes transparent and glassy. This means that you don't have to varnish paintings done in egg tempera—they varnish themselves!

Saponification in Homemade Soap

You Will Need

- 1½ cup (360 ml) lard
- ½ cup (120 ml) olive oil
- Lye flakes or grains
- Large glass casserole dish
- Medium pot
- Large pot
- Glass jar
- Baking pan
- Cellophane wrap
- Measuring cup
- Tablespoon
- Disposable wooden spoon or stirrer
- Electric blender
- Thermometer
- Rubber gloves
- Goggles
- Bottled distilled water

Making soap is easy and fun, but the process requires the use of potentially dangerous materials, so you must take basic precautions. Rubber gloves and goggles are essential. You'll be using lye, a highly alkaline and caustic chemical that's essential to the saponification process. Lye turns fats into fatty acids.

Procedure

1. Half-fill the large pot with tap water and heat until the water temperature is about 95° F (35° C). Place the pot in the sink.

2. In the medium pot, melt 1½ cups (360 ml) of lard over low heat. When the lard is thoroughly liquefied, add ½ cup (120 ml) of olive oil and stir with the wooden spoon.

3. Pour the lard and olive oil into the glass casserole dish, and place the dish into the large pot filled with tap water. Allow the lard and oil mixture to cool in this bath of water for about a half hour, or until the outside of the dish feels warm.

4. Fill the glass jar with ¾ cup (6 fl oz or 180 ml) of cold bottled water. In a well-ventilated place, add 2 tablespoons (30 ml) of lye to the water and stir. Use the stick end of the wooden spoon to stir the lye, and do not breathe the gas that's produced as the lye and water react.

Note: Never use a metal utensil to stir a solution containing lye. The lye will react with the metal and contaminate the solution with lye ions that can be irritating to the skin.

5. Remove the lard-and-oil mixture from the bath and place the casserole dish on a firm, level surface. CAREFULLY add the lye-water to the lard and oil, stirring slowly with the wooden spoon. Notice how the mixture becomes cloudy and begins to thicken. The process of *saponification* has begun as molecules of lye react with fat molecules, breaking them apart.

CAUTION: Avoid splashing any of this solution onto exposed skin. If this happens, stop what you're doing and rinse the exposed area under cold water for a few minutes.

6. Continue stirring the mixture until it turns opaque and begins to look like a runny custard. This is called tracing, and it means that your soap is nearly finished cooking. One way to test whether your soap has traced is to lift the spoon and watch how the string of soap reacts with the surface. If the string leaves little trails on the surface, the soap has thoroughly saponified.

Note: If you stir the soap manually, it can take upwards of an hour before your soap thickens sufficiently. Using an electric blender shortens this time to 15 minutes.

7. Line the baking dish with cellophane wrap and carefully pour the soap into the baking dish. Cover the dish with another sheet of cellophane wrap, and set the soap aside to cool for about 24 hours. The saponification process will continue as the soap cures.

8. After 24 hours, remove the soap from the baking dish and cut it into bars. Stack the bars on a piece of waxed paper and place them in a warm, dry place for at least 2 weeks while the curing continues.

CAUTION: You must allow the soap to cure for several weeks to make sure the alkaline quality of the soap diminishes as saponification continues. If you use the soap before it's ready, it could irritate your skin.

Result

With proper mixing and curing, you will create a fresh-smelling, cream-colored soap that gives a gentle lather while moisturizing your skin with olive oil and glycerine (a chemical byproduct of the saponification process).

Your soap will have a higher water content than commercial soap, and so it may dehydrate if left out in the air. Place each bar in a plastic bag until you're ready to use it.

Explanation

The key to creating soap lies in the chemical properties of lye. This chemical—sodium hydroxide ($NaOH$)—reacts with water in a process called hydrolysis. You may have noticed the water heating up as you added lye to it. This was because the molecules of lye were reacting with the molecules of hydrogen in the water to create a highly alkaline substance. Alkalines have the ability to change fats into fatty acids.

The molecules of fatty acid have the ability to surround particles of fat and debris on your skin and keep them from recombining. This is why washing with soap and rinsing with water cleans you.

Old-Fashioned Fire Extinguisher

If you've ever wandered through an antique shop, you might've seen curious objects that look like glass lightbulbs filled with liquid. Some of them have a separate chamber inside that appears to have held some other substance. These are fire extinguishers from a time when air compression was too difficult and expensive to manufacture commercially.

Their chemistry is simple: Fill a glass bulb with two reacting agents, but keep the agents separated until the bulb is used. During a fire, the user would shake the bulb vigorously to combine the agents. The mixture would fizz and create carbon-dioxide foam that would escape in a spray from one end of the bulb. Carbon dioxide replaces the oxygen a fire needs to continue burning, and so it extinguishes the fire.

You can create a similar device using ordinary household materials.

Procedure

1. Drill a small hole in the center of the bottle's screw top.

2. Using the prong of a fork, carefully pry the staple off a tea bag so you can unfold the bag. (A staple remover might tear it.) Cut the label from the string, but don't remove the string from the tea bag.

3. Cut off the end of the tea bag opposite the string and empty out the tea. Replace the tea with 2 teaspoons (10 ml) of baking soda.

4. Fold the bag in half and hold the halves together with a paper clip.

5. Fill the plastic bottle to the halfway mark with vinegar.

6. Tie the end of the tea-bag string to the neck of the bottle, then carefully push the tea bag into the bottle so that it hangs about 1½ inches (7.5 cm) from the vinegar.

7. Screw the cap on the bottle.

8. When you're ready to test your extinguisher, place your finger over the hole and shake the bottle so that the vinegar saturates the tea bag. The tea bag should open and spill its baking soda into the vinegar. Turn the bottle on its side with the cap facing away from you and remove your finger.

hole in screw cap

tea bag filled with baking soda

vinegar

Old-Fashioned Fire Extinguisher

Result

White foam sprays from the hole in the bottle cap.

Explanation

When combined, alkaline and acid solutions react chemically to create a substance with a neutral PH level. In this case, the alkaline baking soda reacts with the acidic vinegar to produce neutral carbon-dioxide gas. The bubbles of carbon dioxide accumulate with increasing pressure until you release your finger.

Did You Know?

As *pyrotechnology* (the science of fires) became more sophisticated, simple carbon-dioxide extinguishers fell out of use. For one thing, as carbon-dioxide gas replaces oxygen in a closed area, the danger of suffocation exists. Modern extinguishers use highly compressed substances that are effective on many types, or classes, of fire. These include Class A for ordinary combustibles, Class B for flammable liquids, and Class C for combustible metals.

Some elements of the old fire-extinguisher design remain, however. This is why you must always keep a fire extinguisher in an upright position and avoid shaking it until it's needed.

Verdigris, or Copper Oxidation

You Will Need

- Small copper cup or artifact
- Copper-carbonate solution
  (*chemical-supply house*)
- Household ammonia or
  vinegar
- Brass cleaner
- Measuring cup
- Water-misting bottle
- Disposable plastic bucket
- Narrow paintbrush
- Newspapers
- Paper towels

This project shows how you can create a beautiful natural finish on copper called verdigris. *Verdigris,* which means "green of Greece," actually protects copper or brass from the corrosive oils and acids of our environment. This is what distinguishes it from the more common types of rust oxidation. The most dramatic example of verdigris is found on the Statue of Liberty in New York Harbor. The thick verdigris on the statue's copper skin helps protect it from harsh weather and damaging pollutants in the air.

Over time, verdigris forms naturally as a surface is exposed to water vapor containing dissolved chemicals. But you can speed up this process by mixing a solution of ammonia and copper carbonate and brushing it on the item you wish to oxidize. Since brass is a combination of copper and zinc, you can use the solution to create verdigris on brass objects as well as on copper ones.

Procedure

1. Spread the newspaper out on the floor or table to create a working surface.

2. To remove any varnish on the copper or brass, apply a light coating of brass cleaner to the cup with a paper towel. Allow the cleaner to dry; then wipe off the cleaner with a clean paper towel.

3. In the plastic bucket, mix 1 cup (240 ml) of household ammonia with ¼ cup (60 ml) of copper-carbonate solution. If you substitute vinegar, use 2 cups (480 ml) of it undiluted.

CAUTION: Mix in a well-ventilated area and do not breathe the fumes.

4. Dip the brush in the solution, and apply solution to the outside of the cup. Leave the inside uncoated so that you can compare the verdigris with the unoxidized metal.

5. Allow the cup to dry; then brush more of the solution onto the cup. For a deeper green, repeat this procedure five or six times. After the last coat dries, apply a light mist of water to the cup.

Result

A powdery green and bluish coating will appear on the copper. The bluish coating appears where you've misted the surface with water, while the greenish coatings appear in pockets where the solution has concentrated.

Explanation

The mixture of ammonia and copper carbonate, when allowed to air-dry against the copper metal, interacts with copper, air, and water to create the green-colored corrosion. The verdigris consists of a mixture of copper salts including copper sulfate, copper chloride, and copper oxide. Each of the salts is characterized by different sizes of crystals, which create the various green and blue hues.

Immersion Copper Plating

You Will Need

- 20 pennies or copper coins
- Iron nail
- Steel wool
- White vinegar
- Ammonia
- Salt
- Measuring cup
- Teaspoon or 5-ml spoon
- Glass jar
- Plate
- Paper towels

Not all metal plating requires electrical current, as this project will show. Some metals are so active that, when placed in an acetic or salt solution with a less active metal, they naturally lose electrons to the solution. The lost electrons collect and coat the surface of the less active metal in a process called *immersion plating*.

Procedure

1. Fold some sheets of paper towel on a plate. Place the 20 pennies or copper coins on the paper towel. Pour just enough ammonia on the coins to wet them. When the coins dry they will have a green corrosive coating called verdigris.

CAUTION: Pour the ammonia in a well-ventilated area and do not breathe the fumes.

2. Place 1 cup (240 ml) of white vinegar into the glass jar and add ½ teaspoon (2.5 ml) of salt. Stir the salt and vinegar until the salt dissolves.

3. Add 20 pennies or copper coins to the jar. Wait for the verdigris on the coins to disappear so that the true copper color emerges again.

4. Rub the steel wool against the iron nail so that you polish the nail's surface. Then drop the nail into the jar with the copper coins.

5. Leave the jar overnight and check for any changes in the nail the following morning.

Result

The iron nail has a coppery coating on its surface. This coating will deepen the longer you leave the nail in the vinegar-and-salt solution.

Explanation

The combination of vinegar (acetic acid and water) and salt (sodium chloride) dissolves the corrosion (a mixture of copper salts) on the copper coins and allows more copper to make contact with the vinegar-and-salt solution. This is also why you rubbed steel wool on the nail before adding it to the jar.

The steel wool removed any traces of oil or rust from the nail's surface, allowing more of the iron to make contact with the solution. Now both metals are fully exposed to the vinegar and salt, which act on each metal in a different way.

In any kind of plating reaction, the more active metal loses electrons to the less active metal. The solution acts as an electrolyte, which means that it facilitates the movement of electrons from one metal to the other. Of copper and iron, copper is the more active metal, and so it loses electrons more easily. These electrons are forced out of the solution when they reach the nail where they collect and coat the iron surface.

Centrifugal Separation

You Will Need

- Glass test tube with rubber stopper
- Nylon stocking
- 3 rubber bands
- Chalk
- Fine-gauge sandpaper
- Sheet of paper
- Sand
- Orange juice
- Grape juice
- Low-fat milk
- Water

This project demonstrates a technique that involves separating the solid, or particulate, content of a liquid from the liquid itself. Liquids containing particulates are called suspensions. Blood is a suspension, and in hematology (the study of blood), corpuscles are forced from their plasma so that they can be examined and tested more precisely. This is done with a device called a centrifuge. Chemists like the centrifuge because it can force the particulates from a suspension according to density.

Procedure

1. Over a sheet of paper, scrape a piece of chalk against sandpaper until you collect ½ teaspoon (2.5 ml) of chalk dust on the paper.

2. Fold the paper and tap the dust into the test tube. Fill the test tube to the top with water and seal it with the rubber stopper.

3. Push the test tube down into the toe of the nylon stocking. Then wrap rubber bands around the stocking and test tube to keep the test tube upright.

4. Hold the end of the stocking and swing it as fast as you can in a wide circle over your head. Continue swinging for about 2 minutes.

Note: Make sure you have enough room to swing the stocking without hitting something.

5. Carefully remove the test tube from the stocking without shaking it or turning it over. Examine the contents.

6. Repeat steps #1–4, but this time add a pinch of sand along with chalk to the test tube.

7. Wash out the test tube and fill it first with grape juice, then with orange juice, and finally with skim milk. Examine each liquid after spinning.

Result

After 2 minutes of spinning, the chalk collected in a solid layer at the bottom of the test tube. When sand was added, the sand collected at the bottom, followed by a layer of chalk. Of the two juices, orange juice showed the most separation of fruit particulates from water, but grape juice showed separation also. The milk showed no separation at all.

Explanation

The large particles of chalk and sand suspended in water were easily separated out by the centrifugal force of spinning. The sand collected lower than chalk because sand is denser and heavier than chalk. The heavy orange particulates separated from water, as did the particulates of grape in the grape juice. Particles of fat did not separate from milk because the process of homogenization makes fat particles so small that they can't easily be separated. Smaller particles of fat allow people to digest milk more easily.

Recycled Paper: Natural & Bleached

You Will Need

- Stack of old newspapers
- Large (pasta-size) pot
- Medium cooking pot
- Small picture frame (that fits inside large pot)
- 6 rectangular felt pieces, each twice the picture frame's area
- Small piece of screen or fine netting
- Thumbtacks
- Wooden spoon
- Plywood board
- Bleach
- Electric blender (optional)

Paper is an amazingly durable and permanent material. Although most papermakers now use about 30% recycled paper for making new paper, almost all paper can be recycled when processed correctly. However, the bleaching required to make high-quality recycled paper can itself harm the environment, so paper manufacturers are working to find a better solution.

This project takes you through the basic steps of turning old paper into new. Bleaching one batch of paper will allow you to compare the final result.

Procedure

1. Tear a stack of old newspapers into strips and place the strips in the large cooking pot. Fill the pot with water, and allow the strips to soak for about 10 minutes; then pour off the water. This removes the loose printing ink.

2. Use your hands to shred the strips into small pieces. The smaller the pieces, the smoother your paper will be.

3. Add water to the paper so that the shreds are completely covered, and allow the shreds to soak overnight.

4. Boil the newspaper and water until the newspaper dissolves into a kind of thick oatmeal.

Note: If you don't want to boil water, you can just add the paper-and-water mixture to a blender, but this will give you a coarser, weaker paper.

5. Pour half of this mixture into the second medium-size pot and add ½ cup (120 ml) of bleach. Allow the mixture to settle for several hours. A smooth layer of paper pulp will float to the top of the water.

6. Stretch the piece of screen or netting over the picture frame and tack it around the edges.

7. On a flat surface, open the felt and place the plywood board next to it.

8. Carefully dip the picture frame into the soup pot (without the bleach), and lift the frame out so that the mushy pulp forms a sheet on the screen. If you see holes in the sheet, spoon some pulp over them.

9. Let the water drip through the screen and back into the pot. Then move the frame over one side of the piece of felt, and quickly flip the frame over so that the sheet of pulp drops onto the felt.

10. Fold the other side of the felt over the sheet, and place the plywood board on top of the felt.

11. Press down on the board to squeeze excess water out of the paper. Then lift the board and unfold the felt, exposing the paper.

12. Repeat this paper-making process twice more with the other pieces of felt. Then repeat the entire process using the bleached paper mixture.

13. Allow your six pieces of paper to dry overnight; then carefully peel each piece from the felt.

Result

You will have six sheets of a rough but sturdy paper, three sheets of which are a bright whitish-yellow. Your paper may not fold without breaking, however, so test a few pieces before you use it.

Explanation

Paper consists mostly of wood pulp or lignum. When soaked and heated, the pulp breaks apart into tiny fibers that can be mixed around in a kind of paper soup, but they lock together again when the pulp is pressed into a sheet and the water removed.

Professional papermakers add other ingredients to paperlike clays and starches to strengthen the locking of fibers. These bonding agents make the paper stronger, more pliable, and easier to use without crumbling.

CO$_2$ Version of Hero's Engine

You Will Need

- Plastic film canister
- 3 seltzer tablets
- Thread
- Wire hanger
- Styrofoam block (base)
- Drill with 3/32-inch bit
- Masking tape
- Rubber band
- Water

You may remember Hero as the scientist of ancient Greece who invented a spinning engine powered by steam. This version of Hero's engine remains true to the spirit of the original, but uses updated materials in the form of a plastic film canister and two seltzer tablets.

Procedure

1. Straighten a wire hanger, and bend one end of it into a hook. Insert the straight end into the Styrofoam base.

2. Drill a small hole in the side of the film canister close to the top. Then drill a small hole on the opposite side, close to the bottom.

3. Loop a rubber band around the middle of the canister, and attach a piece of thread to the rubber band.

4. Hold the thread to make sure the film case hangs balanced on the thread (you may have to adjust the position of the rubber band). When the canister is balanced, tie the thread to the wire hanger.

5. Tear off a strip of masking tape and have it ready.

6. Remove the cover from the film canister and put in 2 seltzer tablets. Add about 1 tablespoon (15 ml) of water and immediately replace the cap on the canister, securing it with the strip of masking tape.

7. Stand back and observe your engine in motion.

Result

Two jets of gas shoot from the holes in the side of the film canister, causing the case to spin rapidly on the thread.

Explanation

When a seltzer tablet dissolves in water, a chemical reaction takes place. Most seltzer tablets contain a base of sodium bicarbonate (baking soda) and dehydrated citric acid. When you drop the tablet in water, the citric acid combines with the baking soda. Acids and bases undergo a chemical reaction when they mix, producing bubbles filled with carbon-dioxide gas. In the closed film canister, the gases accumulate and create pressure. This pressure eventually escapes as small jets through the holes in the side of the case, causing the canister to rotate.

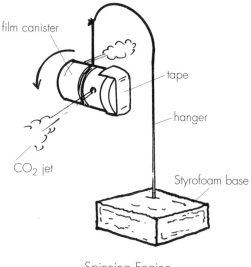

film canister

tape

hanger

CO$_2$ jet

Styrofoam base

Spinning Engine

Essential Oils in Homemade Perfume

You Will Need

- 7 small spice bottles with lids
- Rubbing alcohol
- Cotton swab
- Tweezers
- Zip-top bags
- Tablespoon or 15-ml spoon
- Paper towel
- ⅛ cup (30 ml) each: fragrant rose petals, gardenia blossoms, orange- or lemon-tree leaves, eucalyptus leaves, basil leaves, pine needles
- Masking tape
- Felt-tip marking pen

This project demonstrates one of the oldest uses of chemistry: perfume-making. Early chemists soon realized that, by adding other ingredients to a plant's essential oils, not only could less oil be used, but the essential oil's scent would last longer.

Procedure

1. Fill ⅛ cup (30 ml) with each of the leaf and flower samples. Place each sample into a plastic zip-top bag, and then crush each sample through its bag using the back of a tablespoon.

2. Add 1 teaspoon (5 ml) of rubbing alcohol to each bag and continue crushing.

3. Empty each of the crushed samples into a spice bottle. Screw the lids on the bottles and allow the samples to stand for about a week. Using a marking pen and masking tape, label the bottles.

4. After a week, open one of the bottles and dip in the cotton swab. Lift the swab toward your face, and fan the air around the moist tip so that the odor reaches your nose.

5. Dab the moist tip against the back of your wrist; then allow the spot to dry. Smell it.

6. Use the tweezers to remove a sample of pulverized plant material from one of the bottles. Allow the sample to dry and then smell it.

Result

The moist swab had a strong alcohol scent mixed with the plant scent. After you allowed the liquid to dry on your skin, your skin had only the plant fragrance with no alcohol odor. The dried sample of pulverized plant had no scent at all.

Explanation

Alcohol reacts with the essential oils in plants so that they leech from the plant tissue, enter the alcohol, and remain there until exposed to air. This is why the dried plant sample had no odor but the alcohol contained a fragrance. Alcohol is the perfect "container" for the molecules of essential oils because, when exposed to air, the alcohol dries quickly and leaves only the fragrance of the oil behind.

Protein-Eating Pineapple

You Will Need

- Unflavored (clear) gelatin mix
- 2 heat-tempered glass bowls, same size
- Fresh pineapple

Humans, like all animals, survive by breaking food substances into their simpler components and then absorbing the nutrients. After you eat, the lining of your stomach secretes acids and enzymes that disassemble proteins, carbohydrates, and fats. In this project, you can see one of these powerful enzymes at work by observing the effect of raw pineapple on a bowl of gelatin.

Procedure

1. Mix the gelatin and pour it into the two bowls. Put the bowls in the refrigerator to allow the gelatin to set overnight.

2. Remove the bowls of gelatin. Cut up a raw pineapple and place a small piece of it on top of the gelatin in one of the bowls. Use the rest of the pineapple for fruit salad.

3. Leave the bowls overnight, and then compare the pineapple bowl with the plain gelatin bowl. Record your observations.

Result

The pineapple has dissolved an entire layer of gelatin, turning much of it back into liquid. The gelatin without the pineapple remains firm.

Explanation

Pineapple is one of many fruits that contain a large quantity of proteolytic enzymes. These powerful chemicals have the ability to break down simple proteins. The protein in gelatin takes the form of amino acids, which connect in long chains and give the gelatin its body. Adding a proteolytic enzyme to a gelatin's amino acids breaks the long chains so that the gelatin falls apart.

Separate the Constituents of Table Salt

You Will Need

- Drinking glass
- Table salt
- Tablespoon or 15-ml spoon
- Two 1-foot (30-cm) insulated copper wires
- 6-volt battery
- Scissors

You can easily separate table salt into its constituent elements with the aid of a 6-volt battery. The process not only separates salt, but it allows you to determine the polarity of the battery's voltage by the unique way each element reacts with the copper wire.

Procedure

1. Fill the drinking glass three-fourths full of warm water. Add 3 tablespoons (45 ml) of table salt and stir until the salt dissolves.

2. Use the scissors to strip about 4 inches (10 cm) of insulation from the ends of the copper wires.

3. Attach one end of a wire to the battery's positive terminal and place the other end in the water. Attach one end of the second wire to the battery's negative terminal and place the other end in the water.

4. Leave the wires undisturbed in the water for about 20 minutes and note any changes in the wires.

Result

Tiny bubbles form around one wire while the other wire turns green.

Explanation

The electrical current from the battery, traveling through the wires and into the dissolved salt, breaks the salt molecules into their constituent parts. These parts consist of sodium, a silvery metal, and chloride, a yellowish gas also called chlorine. In the process of splitting the salt, sodium is produced at the negative wire. This sodium easily unites with the water, forming hydrogen gas—the bubbles on the wire. The chlorine is attracted to the positive wire, where it first forms copper chloride and then copper oxide, which colors the wire green.

The polarity of the wires is clearly revealed by the bubbles of hydrogen on the negative wire and the green coating, or verdigris, on the positive wire. As the salt separation continues, hydrogen gas will continue to accumulate in the water, turning it into a caustic soda.

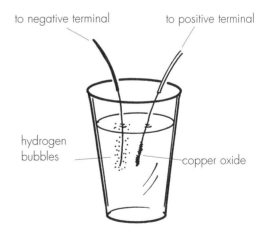

Water-and-Salt Solution

Compare Density & Freezing Temperature

You Will Need

- 3 plastic party glasses, same size
- Sugar
- Salt
- Felt-tip marking pen
  Water

This simple project will help you determine the density of a dissolved solid and the freezing temperature of its solvent. Physicists find that comparing these two factors yields important information about the nature of matter.

Procedure

1. Fill two glasses with water almost to the top. Fill the third glass with water to the top.

2. Add 3 teaspoons (15 ml) of sugar to the first glass and 3 teaspoons (15 ml) of salt to the second glass. Label these glasses SUGAR and SALT. Label the third (full) glass WATER.

3. Place all 3 glasses in the freezer, and check every 2 hours to see which of the three liquids begins to freeze first. Leave all three glasses in the freezer overnight if necessary.

Result

The plain water begins to freeze first, followed by the sugar water. The salt water either takes much longer to freeze than the other two waters, or it doesn't freeze at all.

Explanation

When you dissolve a solid into water, you lower the water's freezing temperature by a degree that's proportional to the density of the dissolved particles. If you double the density of particles in water, you double the amount by which the freezing temperature is lowered. Since you added equal quantities of sugar and salt to the water, you would expect the water's freezing temperature to be lowered equally between the sugar and water solutions. But dissolved salt makes for a much denser solution than dissolved sugar, and the chemical changes that occur as salt dissolves add to this density.

Solid salt (sodium chloride) is almost 40% denser than solid sugar (sucrose) so that 1 teaspoon (5 ml) of salt weighs more than 1 teaspoon (5 ml) of sugar. In addition, a salt molecule weighs only about 8% as much as a sugar molecule, so there are many more salt molecules in a teaspoon of salt than sugar molecules in a teaspoon of sugar.

Finally, when a salt molecule dissolves, it breaks into two electrically charged particles, called *ions*. So for every particle dissolved, two particles form, doubling the density. Sugar molecules remain intact. These interesting properties of salt all contribute to its making a denser solution that requires a colder temperature to freeze.

Triboluminesence in a Life Saver

Certain crystals have inherent electrical properties that, under the proper conditions, can be stimulated. When a crystal such as sugar is broken or fractured, electrical energy is released in the form of light waves. Scientists call this phenomenon *triboluminescence*, which means "rubbing for light." You can see this phenomenon in an ordinary wintergreen Life Saver candy.

Procedure

1. Place a few wintergreen-flavored Life Savers into a small zip-top bag and place the bag into the mortar bowl.

2. Take the bowl into a dark room and allow your eyes to adjust to the dark.

3. Holding the mortar against a firm surface, slowly roll the pestle against the Life Savers, crushing them. You don't have to see precisely where they are to do this.

4. Pick up the bag with the crushed Life Savers and rub the bag so that the pieces of Life Savers scrape against each other.

5. Leave the room, let your eyes readjust, and record your observations.

Result

With each roll of the pestle, the crushed Life Savers emit a tiny burst of white light. Rubbing the crushed pieces together in the bag produces a finer glowing light.

Explanation

Crushing the Life Saver destroys the crystal that was formed when the liquid sugar cooled into a hard candy. Only wintergreen Life Savers have this particular triboluminescent crystalline formation.

You won't find the same reaction with other flavors of Life Savers.

Earth & Sky

Plot Spherical Distance on a Mercator Projection Map

Calculate the Circumference of the Earth

Topographic Mapping of Mountains

Contour-Map a Geological Depression

Measure the Saltation of Sand

Create & Preserve Sand Dunes

How Grain Size Affects Water Absorption

Recreate Natural Abrasion with a Rock Tumbler

Bell Simulation of an Earthquake's S–P Interval

Race for the Epicenter

Vary the Viscosity of Crude Oil

Five Types of Fossilization

Echolocate the Ocean Floor

Plot Spherical Distance on a Mercator Projection Map

This project demonstrates the unavoidable distortions that occur when mapmakers represent the Earth's sphere on a flat surface. We'll measure Earth's circumference distances from the small globe and plot them on a Mercator projection map. This procedure will dramatically highlight both the strengths and weaknesses of the widely used Mercator projection as a representation of the Earth's sphere.

Mapmakers have long struggled with the difficulty of mapping the Earth. To help solve the problem, several types of map projection have been developed. Each projection is useful for a particular kind of information, and each is designed to confine distortion to areas unrelated to the map's main purpose.

3 Types of Map Projection

Projections that are taken from one of the Earth's poles and radiate outward from the poles are called gnomic. A *gnomonic projection* maintains the straight lines of longitude

so that the shortest distance between two locations can be measured accurately. However, since the lines of latitude are curved, gnonomic projections are not very useful for determining direction. In addition, gnonomic projections can only be made for one hemisphere at a time, and distortion increases in areas farthest from the poles.

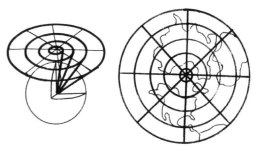

Gnomic-Projection Map

Polyconic projections are more accurate for direction because the lines of longitude are straight and the lines of latitude have only a slight curve. This means that both direction and distance can be calculated with reasonable accuracy. The drawback of polyconic projections is that they can only show a relatively small area of the Earth's surface and so are not useful for long-distance navigation.

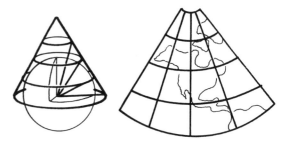

Polyconic-Projection Map

Mercator projections, named after the Dutch mapmaker Gerardus Mercator (1512–1594), offer the best compromise. To understand how a Mercator map is created, imagine a piece of paper wrapped around a globe at its equator. Imaginary lines from the center of the globe pass through the surface and onto the paper. As you can see from the illustration, these lines spread far apart before they reach the paper, and this creates distortions in the sizes of land formations, particularly near the poles.

On a Mercator projection map, Greenland appears roughly the size of South America, when it is actually only one-fifth its size. But because a Mercator projection has perfectly straight lines of longitude and latitude, it's as accurate as a gnomonic projection for distances, and improves upon the direction-finding advantages of polyconic projections.

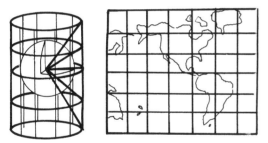

Mercator-Projection Map

Latitudinal Distortion

1. Measure and cut a length of string 20 cm (8 inches) longer than the circumference of your globe. Mark the string at intervals of 2 cm (⅘ inch) all along its length. Wrap the string around the globe at the equator and tie it tightly.

2. Carefully slide the string until one of the marks lies where the equator and prime meridian cross just off the southern coast of Ghana, Africa (latitude 0°, longitude 0°). Using one of the colored pencils, mark that same location on the Mercator projection map.

3. Choose a place on the globe beneath one of the marks on the string. Determine the longitude and latitude of that place. Find the same longitude and latitude on the Mercator projection and mark it with the pencil. Repeat this procedure for every mark on the string.

4. Connect all the adjacent points on the Mercator projection map with the colored pencil and observe the shape of your line.

Longitudinal Distortion

1. Slide the string perpendicularly so that it now covers a line of longitude.

2. Moving longitudinally, choose a place on the globe beneath one of the marks on the string. Determine the longitude and latitude of that place and mark it on the Mercator projection map. Repeat this procedure for every mark on the string.

3. Connect all adjacent points on the map and observe your line.

Transverse Distortion

1. Move the tied string back to its original equatorial position. Take the two free pieces of string and hold them at a 45-degree angle to the equatorial string. Use a little tape to join the strings together at the opposite side of the globe and fix the strings in position.

2. As before, choose a place on the globe beneath each of the marks and replicate that position's longitude and latitude on the Mercator projection map. Connect the adjacent points with colored pencil.

Result

Each line you drew on the Mercator projection map highlights the map's strengths and weaknesses in representing spherical distances. The line tracing equatorial latitude shows the least distortion, while the line tracing longitude shows the most, particularly as you move away from the equator and toward the poles. The transverse line shows a constant but less severe distortion than that of the longitudinal line.

Calculate the Circumference of the Earth

You Will Need

- Removable broomstick from a push broom
- Large metal binder clip
- Small fishing weights
- Tape measure
- Scientific calculator (not business)
- String
- Chalk

Note: Since this project requires the cooperation of two teams- (one in a distant town), you will need two of each item in the "You Will Need" list. Make a second measuring staff just like the first one.

We owe the first accurate calculation of the Earth's circumference to the Greek astronomer Eratosthenes (276–194 B.C.), who was the chief librarian at the great library of Alexandria. By comparing the length and angles of shadows in Alexandria with those in the city of Syene 500 miles (800 km) away, Eratosthenes was able to calculate that the distance between the two cities represented about 1/50th of the distance around the Earth.

This project approximates Eratosthenes' experiment with a pair of measuring staffs and the added convenience of a modern scientific calculator.

Making the Measuring Staff

Procedure

1. Measure and cut a length of string. The string should be three-fourths as long its pole.

2. Tie one end of the string to the fishing weight. Tie the other end of the string to the binder clip.

3. Attach the binder clip to the top of the broomstick.

4. At midday, hold the broomstick upright in the bright sunlight so that the plumb line is parallel to the stick. Have your teammate check the line against the stick from several sides to make sure that the stick isn't leaning.

Synchronized Measurement

Procedure

1. The team in the distant town should be equally equipped and prepared to take a measurement.

2. At a given signal, perhaps a phone call, your team and the distant team must measure the shadow thrown on the ground by the broomstick. Allow the measurer to crouch down and make a chalk mark at the shadow's end while the staff holder remains motionless. (See drawing below.)

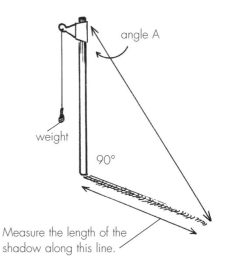

Measuring Staff

3. Using the tape measure, the measurer records the length of the shadow from the base of the pole to the chalk mark.

Making the Calculation

Procedure

1. First, both teams need to work out the sun's angle from their measurements. To do this, divide the length of the shadow by the length of the stick. This gives you the tangent of angle A. To find the sun's angle from this tangent, press the tangent function *(tan)* of the calculator.

2. Compare the angles between the teams. Subtract the smaller angle of one team from the larger angle of the other team. The result is the difference.

Divide 360 (the total number of degrees in the circumference of a circle) by this difference. The result of this division is called the quotient.

Multiply the quotient by the distance between the two teams. Then divide this large number by pi (3.142).

As an example, let's use two teams 500 miles (800 km) apart. If the difference in their angles is 7 degrees, the calculation would be:

$$360° \div 7° = 51.42$$
$$51.42 \times 500 = 25,710 \text{ miles } (41,136 \text{ km})$$
$$25,710 \text{ miles} \div 3.142 = 7,855.2 \text{ miles}$$
$$(13,092 \text{ km})$$

Or,

$$41,136 \text{ km} \div 3.142 = 13,092 \text{ km}$$
$$(7,855.2 \text{ miles})$$

Topographic Mapping of Mountains

You Will Need

- 2 pounds (about 1 kg) of light-colored modeling clay
- Clear plastic storage or sweater box (without lid)
- Clear acrylic sheet, big enough to fit over top
- Large sheet tracing paper
- Grease pencil
- Metric ruler
- Felt-tip marking pen
- Black tempera paint
- Paper paint bucket
- Water
- Sponge

If you live near a mountain, you see one kind of landscape. If you live near the coast, you see another kind of landscape. And if you live in a flat prairie region, you see still another sort of landscape. Topography describes what geologists call the "lay of the land," or the various elevations among diverse landscapes. In this project you will make a mountain range from clay and then create a topographical map of it.

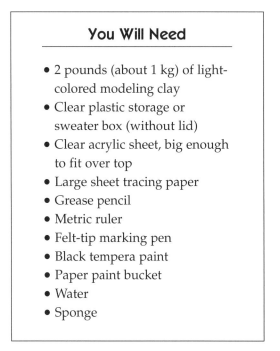

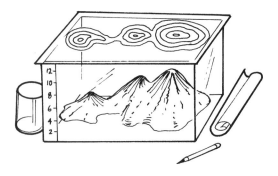

Procedure

1. Using the metric ruler and a grease pencil, make marks up the side of the storage box 2 cm (⅘ inch) apart. Place the box on the floor.

2. Create several mountains of various sizes from the clay, and then connect them with the remaining clay to form a mountain range. Place the mountain range in the box, making sure it fits comfortably and doesn't stick out over the top. The floor of the box represents sea level, or 0 centimeters.

3. Place the acrylic sheet over the top of the box and look down directly through it to your mountain range.

4. Use the grease pencil to trace the widest outline of the mountain range, that is, the mountain range at sea level. The tracing makes an elongated loop called a contour line.

5. Place a sheet of tracing paper over the grease-pencil contour line you just made and trace it with the felt-tip marking pen.

6. Remove the tracing paper and wipe the grease pencil from the acrylic sheet with the sponge.

7. Mix black tempera paint and water in the paper bucket until you get an inky-water effect.

8. Add the inky water to the box up to the 2-cm (⅘-inch) mark.

9. Place the acrylic sheet over the top of the box and, looking down through it again, trace a second contour line where the water meets the clay.

10. Place the tracing paper over the acrylic so that the second contour line fits inside the first. Trace the second contour line.

11. Add inky water to the box up to the 4-cm (1¾-inch) mark, repeating the tracing procedure, until the water level reaches the top of your mountain range.

12. Since we used only a metric ruler for our initial measurement, we now need to translate those measurements into a scale that's more geologically appropriate. Use the scale 2 cm = 10 meters.

(That's ⅘ inch = 400 inches, or 33 feet ³⁄₁₀ inches. Note that 1 meter = 39 to 40 inches.)

13. Write each meter elevation number beside the appropriate contour line on your map, and total the number of meters. Multiply the total number of meters by 3.3 to find the height of your mountain range in feet.

Result

Depending on the depth of your box, you should have a contour map of many concentric contour lines representing the various elevations of your mountain range.

Explanation

The contour lines of topological maps help geologists imagine three-dimensional areas on two-dimensional surfaces. A contour line can meander for many miles and in many directions, but it will always close in a loop since it joins all points of the same elevation. Elevation is expressed as a distance either above or below sea level. The difference in elevation between two adjacent contour lines is called the contour interval, which is usually expressed in even numbers or as a multiple of five.

The size of the chosen contour interval depends on how much the elevation changes in the arcs mapped. For example, to avoid too many contour lines, a high mountain would use a large contour interval. The more gently sloping coastal ranges would use smaller contour intervals.

Display your contour map alongside the model of your mountain range. Create several additional elevations in clay and make contour maps of them, experimenting with various contour-interval scales.

Contour-Map a Geological Depression

You Will Need

- 4 colors of modeling clay
- Clear plastic storage or sweater box (without lid)
- Clear acrylic sheet, big enough to fit over top
- Large sheet of tracing paper
- Grease pencil
- Plastic knife
- Metric ruler
- Sponge
- Felt-tip marking pen

A geological depression is a surface feature that exists below the surface. As defined by geologists, *surface* means "sea level." Like mountains, hills, mesas, and plateaus, depressions are represented in any good elevation or topological map. Depressions come in many varieties, from shallow basins to deep canyons. In this project you will make a deep depression from clay and then record its features by creating a topographical map.

Procedure

1. Make a mountain by layering each color of clay over the other. Each layer should be about 2 cm (⅘ inch) thick. Don't smear the clay together, and shave some clay from the sides of the mountain to give it better shape.

2. Place the box on the floor, then turn the mountain upside down and place it in the box. You may have to flatten the top a little to keep the mountain from falling over. Your mountain is now a depression.

3. Place the metric ruler beside the depression and take a measurement in centimeters. Hold the ruler beside the box and use the grease pencil to make hatch marks 2 cm (⅘ inch) apart up the side of the box until you reach the measurement of the depression.

4. Label the highest hatch mark 0 for sea level, then label the remaining hatch marks 2 cm, 4 cm, 6 cm (⅘ inch, 1¾ inches, 2⅖ inches) as you move down the side of the box.

5. Place the acrylic sheet over the top of the box and look directly down through it.

6. Use the grease pencil to trace the widest outline of the depression. This is the depression at 0 elevation or sea level. Your tracing should make an elongated loop called a contour line.

7. Place a sheet of tracing paper over the grease-pencil contour line you just made and trace it with the marker.

8. Remove the tracing paper and wipe the grease pencil from the acrylic sheet with the sponge.

9. Carefully peel the first layer of clay from the depression so that the second layer of clay is exposed.

Contour Map with Geological Depressions

10. Place the acrylic sheet over the top of the box and, looking down through it again, trace a second contour line around the new color of clay.

11. Place the tracing paper over the acrylic so that the second contour line fits inside the first. Trace the second contour line.

12. Peel a layer of clay away to reveal the next layer, each time tracing a new contour line, first with the grease pencil on the acrylic sheet and then with the marker on the tracing paper.

13. Since we used only a metric ruler for our initial measurement, we now need to translate these measurements into a scale that's more geologically appropriate. Use the scale 2 cm = 10 meters.

(That's ⅘ inch = 400 inches, or 33 feet ³⁄₁₀ inches. Note that 1 meter = 39.37 inches, often rounded off to 39 or 40 inches.)

14. Mark each meter elevation beside the appropriate contour line on your tracing-paper map and total the number of meters. Multiply this total by 3.3 to find the depth of the depression in feet.

Result

Your topological depression map should consist of 4 looped contour lines with the smallest loop indicating the depression's deepest point and the largest loop indicating sea level.

Explanation

Contour lines are an essential part of any topological map because they help geologists represent three-dimensional areas on two-dimensional surfaces. A contour line can meander for many miles and in many directions, but it will always close in a loop since it joins all points of the same elevation.

The difference in elevation between two adjacent contour lines is called the contour interval, which is usually expressed in even numbers or as a multiple of five. The size of the chosen contour interval depends on how much the elevation changes in the areas mapped. For example, to avoid too many contour lines, a deep canyon (such as those found in oceans) would use a large contour interval while more gently sloping coastal basins would use smaller contour intervals.

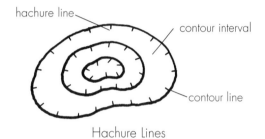

Hachure Lines

Since the contour interval is always a positive number, how do geologists show that a particular contour line indicates depth rather than height? If you look at a detailed topographical map, you'll see that some contour lines have short lines, like dashes, at right angles to the contour line. These hachure (ha SHOOR) lines are used to show areas below sea level. Knowing this, you can now add hachure lines to your topographical map.

Measure the Saltation of Sand

You Will Need

- Plastic ice-cube tray
- Floor tile or small acrylic sheet
- Natural sand (coarse)
- Beach sand (medium)
- Aquarium sand (fine)
- Hair dryer
- Stack of books
- Cup
- Teaspoon or 5-ml spoon
- Magnifying glass

In this project you'll examine how grain size affects the movement of sand to form distinct landscapes.

Wind plays a major role in creating sand features, and this wind-against-sand effect is called saltation. Some sand features are easily recognizable, like the dunes of deserts. But airborne particles accumulate everywhere. The lightest of these—dust particles—are continually suspended in the air by the push of upward air currents. Most dust is deposited only during precipitation.

Also very fine are the lightweight particles called *loess* (LESS) that come from deserts, dry riverbeds, and old glacial lake beds. Loess consists of angular particles that can travel very far and tend to pack together into a dense mass.

In North America, loess deposits are found on hilltops and in valleys near the Mississippi River. This material was carried by the strong winds that blew from the ice sheet that once covered the northern United States and Canada. Loess deposits in China are windblown material from the Gobi and Ordos Deserts.

Saltation Demonstration

Sand dunes are the most common type of wind deposit. Dunes are found in arid and semi-arid regions and along the shores where sand is plentiful. The way they form depends on both the weight of the sand grain and the topographical characteristics of the area. Dunes take on a particular shape from the natural motion of sand against itself and from the distribution of sand grains when blown by wind.

Procedure

1. Mix the coarse, medium, and fine sand in the cup.

2. Place the floor tile on a book, and place the end of the plastic ice-cube tray next to the tile. The tile should be at the same level as the top of the ice-cube tray. You may need to add more books to the tile or tray.

3. Spoon enough sand on the tile to make a small "sand dune." Make sure the dune comes all the way to the edge of the tile, near the ice-cube tray.

4. Turn on the hair dryer and hold it about 5 inches (12.5 cm) from the sand dune. Try to keep it steady for about 30 seconds.

5. Turn off the hair dryer and examine the

sand that has blown into the various compartments of the ice-cube tray. Use the magnifying glass to get a better look.

Result

The compartments closest to the hair dryer contain the coarsest grains of sand. The compartment farthest from the sand dune contains the finest grains of sand. Grains of increasing fineness are contained between the closest and farthest compartments.

Explanation

The finer grains of sand weigh the least and so travel the farthest. The coarser grains weigh more and don't travel as far. This means that, as wind sweeps across a dune, the heavier sand falls steeply down the leeward side of the dune while the lighter materials accumulate in a gentle slope on the windward side of the dune. This dynamic gives the dune its characteristic "wave" shape.

Create & Preserve Sand Dunes

You Will Need

- 5 shallow box lids
- Ruler, yardstick, or meterstick
- Measuring cup
- 1 pound (450 g) medium-grain beach sand
- 1 pound (450 g) fine-grain aquarium sand
- Packet of medium-size aquarium gravel
- Large bucket
- Garden trowel
- Drinking straw
- Spray varnish

In this project, you'll create an approximation of the five common types of sand dune and preserve them for display. Sand dunes, the most common type of wind deposit, are found in arid and semi-arid regions and along the shores where sand is plentiful. Dunes take on particular characteristics depending on several factors. These factors include the amount of vegetation or rock formations in the terrain, the constancy and direction of wind, and the amount of free sand available. The five common dune types are found throughout the world.

Preparing the Terrain

Procedure

1. Remove 5 cups (1.2 L) of sand from the medium sand and 5 cups (1.2 L) of sand from the fine sand. Mix the sands together, separate into two equal containers, and place the containers aside.

2. Combine the remaining medium and fine sand in the large bucket. Use the garden trowel to stir the sands until they are well mixed.

3. Cover the surface of a table with newspaper; then place the box lids on the table. Label the lids 1–5 on the lid flaps.

4. Fill the lids with the mixed sand. Scrape the ruler across the top of each lid to level and smooth the sand.

5. Add three lines of gravel to lid #3, dividing the sand into four columns.

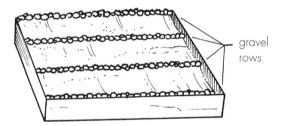

gravel rows

6. Hold the varnish over lids 4 and 5 and carefully spray the surface until the sand grains appear coated. Make sure you don't spray too close and disturb the smoothness of the sand. Put these lids aside to dry.

Dune-Making

Procedure

1. Start with lid #1. Place your face level to the lid and, using the straw, blow carefully and steadily across the sand. Move the straw

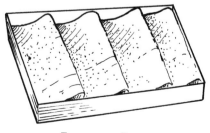

Transverse Dunes

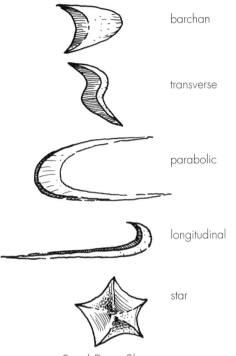

barchan

transverse

parabolic

longitudinal

star

Sand Dune Shapes

After the second ridge forms, turn the lid again. Continue turning and blowing until a star dune appears at the center of the lid.

3. Move to lid #3 and place your face level to the sand, looking down the columns you made with the gravel. Blow gently and steadily in one direction, just as you did for lid #1. The sand will scoop out in the columns and form long horns over the gravel. These parabolic dunes form where certain topographical features, like vegetation or rocks, prevent the formation of the more usual transverse dune.

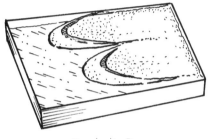

Parabolic Dunes

gently from side to side so that you create the effect of a wide swath of wind. Continue until you create long ridges that slope gently upward on the windward side and drop sharply down on the leeward side. If you're not successful on the first try, smooth the sand with the ruler and begin again. Eventually, several transverse dunes will appear in the sand.

2. Move to lid #2. Place your face level to the lid and blow through the straw. This time, keep the straw steady and blow toward the center of the lid. When you see a small ridge forming at the center, turn the lid one-quarter around and continue blowing.

4. Move to lid #4, the first of the varnished sands. Take the first container of sand you put aside and carefully sprinkle it on the surface. Make sure the hard varnished sand surface is completely covered by the free sand.

5. Using the second container of sand you put aside, repeat this procedure for lid #5.

6. Place your face level to lid #4, and blow as you did for lid #3—that is, across imaginary columns of sand. Soon crescent-shaped (barchan) dunes will appear as free sand moves across the hardened sand beneath it. Barchan dunes are common where free sand is scarce. Continue blowing and you'll see your barchan dunes creep forward.

Star Dune

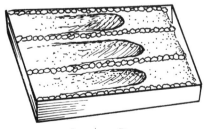

Barchan Dunes

7. Move to lid #5 and blow wide swaths across the sand in one direction. With a little practice, a typical longitudinal or linear dune will appear. These dunes also appear where scarce free sand sits atop packed sand. Steady winds, often spiraling into eddies between the dunes, create dunes that sometimes stretch for hundreds of miles.

8. After you've created a clear example of each dune type, preserve your dunes by using more spray varnish. Carefully move the lids to a well-ventilated place. Hold the varnish at a distance of about 18 inches (45 cm) above each lid and spray evenly, using a sweeping motion.

Allow the varnish to dry overnight and then spray again. The hard varnish coating over your dunes should preserve them and allow you to move them (carefully!) to their display area.

CAUTION: Ventilate the room well to avoid breathing in fumes from the varnish.

How Grain Size Affects Water Absorption

You Will Need

- Three 250-ml beakers
- 250-ml or larger measuring cup
- Package of dried split peas
- Medium-size gravel
- Marbles
- Water

This project compares the absorption capacity of three porous materials with different grain sizes. The intent is to examine which material has the greater capacity to hold water.

It may surprise you to learn that the Earth has much more groundwater than surface water. On the Earth's surface, water travels in rivers or streams. But underground water can travel in streams too, and the movement of this mineral-laden water can create beautiful caverns as it carves hollow pockets in the Earth's crust.

Most underground water collects in natural reservoirs called water tables. To understand how water can accumulate underground, geologists study various materials to determine each material's capacity to store water.

The term *porous* refers to a material that has spaces or pores between its grains. Soils, gravel, and sands are porous. The more general term *permeable* refers to any material that can hold water, such as cracked rocks.

Filling the Gaps

Procedure

1. Fill each beaker to the 200-ml mark with the peas, gravel, and marbles. These materials represent sediment grains. In the grain-volume column of the Absorption Data Table, write "200 ml" beside each material.

2. Pour 250 ml water into the measuring cup. You may find that the water level bulges in the cup a little, making an accurate measurement more difficult. But this effect, called a *meniscus,* won't affect your result.

3. Carefully pour water from the measuring cup into the beaker containing the peas. Stop pouring when the water just covers the peas.

4. Notice the amount of water left in the measuring cup. Record this amount and subtract it from 200 ml. The difference tells you how much water it took to fill all the pores between the peas. Write this figure in the pore-volume column of the data table.

5. Repeat steps #3 and 4 for the remaining beakers.

Calculating Pore Space

Procedure

1. For each grain size—peas, gravel, and marbles—divide pore volume by grain volume.

2. Multiply each decimal figure by 100 to express it as a percentage.

3. Record each percentage in the Pore

Space column of the Data Table, and compare data to determine which material has the greatest pore volume.

Result

The marbles have the greatest pore space (38%) and the peas have the least (25%). We can say that the larger the grain size of a volume, the greater its percentage of pore space, and the more water it can contain.

Explanation

The smaller and more tightly a material's grains pack together, the more the material resembles a nonpermeable solid. Large grains create large pores between them because the grains are under less pressure and can pack together more loosely.

Did You Know?

Some stones, like limestone and sandstone, can actually behave as sponges. Limestone is an excellent container for water and sandstone often contains liquid resources such as crude oil. Since oil is lighter than water, it creeps upward through soft sandstone until it reaches a nonpermeable mantle of shale. The oil collects there for hundred of years and forms a rich deposit.

	Abrasion Data Table		
Grain Size	Grain Volume (ml)	Pore Volume (ml)	Pore Space (percentage)
Small			
Medium			
Large			

Recreate Natural Abrasion with a Rock Tumbler

You Will Need

- Aluminum foil
- Plaster of paris
- Bucket and stirrer
- Large glass jar with lid
- Diatomaceous earth
  (*pool-supply store*)
- Sand
- Thick plastic trash bag
- Towel
- Hammer
- Large piece of poster board
- Yellow food coloring
- Felt-tip marking pen
- Ruler
- Carpenter's glue

The smooth rocks you see at the beach or in a riverbed are the product of a long and violent history. The natural abrasion of water against rocks, or of rocks against themselves as they are swept in a current, is an amazingly powerful force. Even the wind can wear a rock away, and the strong shearing winds found in some deserts have made unusual aeolian (shaped-by-wind) rock formations that seem to defy gravity.

You can simulate the natural abrasion of rocks with a rock tumbler. In this project, you'll also create the rocks, since the abrasion of genuine rocks would take many weeks of constant motion. To make the result as close to real life as possible, you will make two types of rock and compare how each wears down.

Making Rocks

Procedure

1. Copy the Abrasion Table onto the large piece of poster board.

2. Mix the plaster and water in a bucket until you have a thick, puttylike material.

3. Spill half of this mixture onto a piece of aluminum foil.

4. Carefully add 1 cup (240 ml) of diatomaceous earth to the remaining plaster in the bucket and stir. Add yellow food coloring to the mixture.

Abrasion Table

Type	Now	5 minutes	10 minutes	15 minutes	20 minutes
Clastic					
Sedimentary					

5. Spill this mixture onto a second piece of foil.

6. Allow both to harden overnight.

7. When the plaster is thoroughly dry, remove the plain plaster piece and place it in the plastic garbage bag. Put a towel over the bag and use the hammer to crush the piece into smaller pieces. Your pieces should be no more than 1 inch (2.5 cm) in diameter.

8. Repeat this procedure for the plaster mixed with diatomaceous earth.

Rock Polishing

Procedure

1. Choose 20 well-shaped "stones" from each bag and put them in the glass jar. (Reject stones that are too flat.)

2. Add water to the jar to the halfway point and add 1 teaspoon (5 ml) of sand.

3. Shake the jar in all directions, turning it around as you shake it. Continue shaking for 5 minutes, then stop shaking and remove three white stones and three yellow stones.

4. Dry the stones and glue them into the first column of the Abrasion Table.

5. Shake the jar another 5 minutes, then stop and remove three of each type of stone again. Dry the stones and glue them into the second column of the table.

6. Repeat steps #3 and 4 after shaking the jar for another 5 minutes, and then for another 5 minutes after that, so that your final collection represents stones after 20 minutes of shaking.

7. Examine and compare all the stones on the Abrasion Table. Is there a difference in shape between the white stones and yellow stones?

Result

It's generally true that longer periods of shaking resulted in smoother stones. However, the yellow stones (with added diatomaceous earth) are uniformly smoother than those made of plain plaster.

Explanation

When you added diatomaceous earth to the second batch of plaster, you created a type of stone called a clastic. Geologists classify clastics as sedimentary because they are formed by the settling and compression of various materials such as the microscopic fragments of shells. Sedimentary rocks are soft and easily eroded. This is why the yellow stones responded so well to the abrasiveness of the other stones and sand.

The plain plaster stones simulate limestone, one of the non-clastic precipitates. These stones are created when chemical reactions form a solid that settles out of a solution. The hardening of plaster simulates this process. Precipitates are much harder than sedimentary stones, and this accounts for their rougher appearance, even after 20 minutes of tumbling.

Bell Simulation of an Earthquake's S–P Interval

You Will Need

- 4 players
- Wall-size regional map with distance scale bar
- Standard-size regional map with distance scale bar
- 3 pencil compasses
- 3 metric rulers
- Desk bell
- Felt-tip marking pen

This project uses a series of bell rings to simulate how seismologists analyze an earthquake's shockwave to determine epicenter. When an earthquake occurs, it generates an expanding shockwave from its epicenter at a speed of several kilometers a second (1 kilometer = 0.6 mile).

Each seismic station within a wide network of stations detects the shockwave at different times. The information is compiled and examined at one master station.

A Closer Look at Shockwaves

The speed of a shockwave is not constant but varies with many factors, including the depth of the wave's origin and the type of rock it must travel through. However, seismologists have worked out a system that factors in these variables and provides a reasonably accurate result.

They recognize that a shockwave consists of two very distinct wave types, the primary (P) wave and the secondary (S) wave. Taken together, these waves provide and important piece of information called the *S–P interval*.

The S–P Interval

The P and S waves have different attributes. The P wave travels longer and farther because it can penetrate both solids and liquids. This means that it can move through the Earth's core and be detected on the opposite side of its origin. The S wave can penetrate solids only and so travels only half the distance of the P wave. However, the primary wave is always followed by the secondary wave, and the amount of time between the two waves, called the S–P interval, allows for the calculation of epicentral distance—or the distance of the station from the quake's epicenter. The longer the S–P interval, the greater the distance between quake and station.

Sharing Circles

Epicentral distance is represented as the radius of a circle with the station at the center. From the station's point of view, the Earthquake could have occurred at any point along the circle's perimeter. This is why sharing epicentral distance information with two other stations is so important, as you'll see.

We decided that this project would work best as a team effort to give some idea of the quick thinking and cooperation required by seismologists throughout the world.

Preparing for the Big One

Consulting his map, the "Quakemaster" determines the secret location of the earthquake and records longitude and latitude. He then chooses the location of three seismic stations and assigns a station to each player. Stations should be within a 500-mile (800-km) radius of the earthquake. Players mark their stations on the wall map.

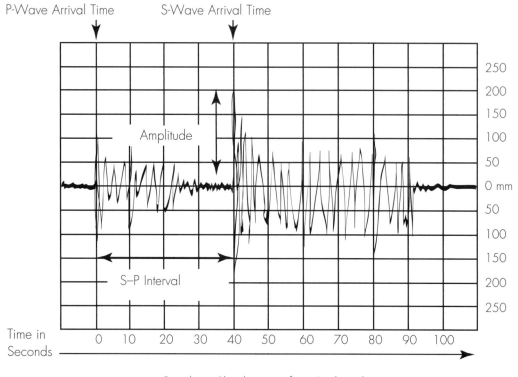

P-Wave Arrival Time   S-Wave Arrival Time

Amplitude

S–P Interval

Time in
Seconds

250
200
150
100
50
0 mm
50
100
150
200
250

0   10   20   30   40   50   60   70   80   90   100

Graphing Shockwave of an Earthquake

In order to time the S–P interval accurately, the Quakemaster must first figure out the distances between stations and earthquake. He does this by using his map scale and translating each distance into a time interval. The formula used is 10 seconds per 100 kilometers (62.14 miles).

For example, if the quake's secret location is Los Angeles and Station A is in Las Vegas, Nevada, the distance between the two places is 400 km (248 miles, or about 250 miles) and the S–P interval is 40 seconds. If Station B is in Tonopah, Nevada, the distance from the quake is 475 km (295 miles, or about 300 miles) and the S–P interval is 47 seconds. If Station C is in Reno, Nevada, the distance is 650 km (403 miles, or about 400 miles) and the interval is 65 seconds.

Knowing these S–P intervals, the Quakemaster can time his bell to accurately represent an expanding shockwave as it passes through each station.

Shockwave!

The Quakemaster rings the bell, indicating the P wave, and this signals each station to start its stopwatch. If we continue the previous example, the next ring occurs 40 seconds later and indicates the S wave passing through Station A (Las Vegas). Seven seconds later, the bell rings again for Station B (Tonopah), and 18 seconds after that it rings again for Station C (Reno). Each station stops its watch at the appropriate ring and records its unique S–P interval.

Equipped with only an S–P interval, each station must now deduce distance by using the graph below—in effect, reversing step #2 of the Quakemaster.

Let's continue with Station A in the previous example. Since the interval for Station A is 40 seconds, the graph translates this into 400 kilometers (248 miles, or almost 250 miles).

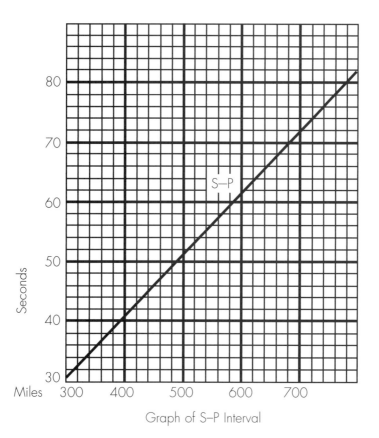

Graph of S–P Interval

Using the bar measurement, each station scales its distance to the wall map and adjusts the angle of its compass to reflect this distance. Station A would adjust the angle of its compass to reflect a distance of 400 kilometers (250 miles).

Each station draws a circle on the wall map with the station's city at the center of the circle. Station A would draw a circle with Las Vegas at the center. The radius of this circle represents 400 kilometers and, from Station A's point of view, the quake could have occurred anywhere along the circumference of the circle. Stations B and C would follow suit, each drawing a circle with a radius equaling the distance calculated from the S–P interval. The radius for Station B's circle would represent 475 km (294.5 miles, or nearly 300 miles) and the radius for Station C's circle would represent 650 km (403 miles, just over 400 miles).

Stations triangulate their circles to determine the epicenter of the quake and discover its secret location. In other words, after completing the three circles, the players look for a point where all three circles intersect. They record the longitude and latitude coordinates at the location and compare them with the Quakemaster's coordinates.

Did You Know?

A *seismograph* is an instrument simple in concept but one that must be designed and set up very carefully. The three basic parts of the seismograph are the beam, the rotating drum, and the drum support. The drum support rests on the Earth's bedrock, or the solid rock beneath the soil. During an earthquake, the support moves, moving the attached drum. However, a pen hanging from the beam remains stationary and records the drum's movements. The pen marks a piece of graph paper attached to the drum. This paper indicates both the time and the wave size in millimeters.

Race for the Epicenter

In this project you and your friends will use the technique of epicentral triangulation to determine the location and direction of an earthquake.

When an earthquake occurs, it generates an expanding shockwave from its epicenter at a speed of several kilometers a second. This shockwave is detected at different times by each seismic station within a wide network of stations. A seismic station estimates its distance from the origin of the quake by dividing the shockwave into two parts—the primary (P) and secondary (S) wave. Each station measures how quickly the S wave follows the P wave, and the resulting time interval is used to calculate the station's *epicentral distance.*

Epicentral distance is represented as the radius of a circle with the station at its center. To triangulate a quake's location, the first three stations to detect the shockwave share their epicentral distances so that three circles can be drawn. The epicenter of the Earthquake is the point where all three circles intersect.

This project takes a shortcut through P-wave and S-wave calculations in order to clearly demonstrate the technique of epicentral triangulation. The game format allows a "Quakemaster" to choose a secret location for the earthquake and challenge three seismic stations to find the quake's epicenter.

Procedure

1. Each of three players chooses a location for his seismic station and marks it on his map. The first player to choose shares his location so that the others can place their stations within a 500-mile (800-km) radius. Each player knows the location of the other players and marks it on the map.

2. The Quakemaster decides where the earthquake will occur, marking the map and recording the longitude and latitude. Using the map's scale bar and a metric ruler, he calculates the distance of the quake from each of the three seismic stations (epicentral distance).

3. Each station writes down all three epicentral distances, provided by the Quakemaster in kilometers.

4. On the Quakemaster's direction "LOCATE," each station adjusts its compass

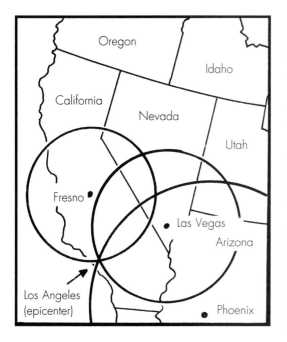

Triangulation Method for Locating
Quake Epicenter

so that the distance between the point and pencil equals its unique epicentral distance.

5. Each station places the needle of its compass at the location of its station on the map. It sweeps the pencil around to make a circle around the station.

6. Each station repeats this procedure for the remaining stations, ending up with three circles of different sizes.

7. The point where all three circles intersect is the epicenter of the earthquake. The first station to correctly call out the longitude and latitude of the earthquake's epicenter wins the game.

Did You Know?

The most severe earthquake in American history was actually a series of earthquakes that began on December 16, 1811, and lasted until March of 1812. Known as the New Madrid Earthquakes, they shook more than two-thirds of the United States and were felt as far away as Canada. The strongest quake had its epicenter in New Madrid, Missouri. It changed the level of land by as much as 20 feet (6 m), altered the course of the Mississippi River, and created brand-new lakes, such as Lake St. Francis in Tennessee.

Vary the Viscosity of Crude Oil

You Will Need

- 100-ml graduated cylinder
- Plastic window-cleaner bottle with spray pump
- Plastic tubing to fit into spray pump
- Aquarium gravel
- Vegetable oil
- Hot and cold water
- Dishwashing liquid detergent

This project demonstrates how certain techniques can lower the viscosity of petroleum so that it can be pumped from its hiding places and brought to the surface. Although rich deposits of petroleum exist underground, getting this crude oil to the surface can be extremely difficult. Even pumps capable of thousands of pounds of pressure have difficulty extracting oil that remains locked in layers of permeable sandstone or hidden in the cracks of rocks.

To make things even more difficult, petro-leum, like all other liquids, has an internal friction that affects its rate of flow. This friction is called viscosity, and crude oil has an extremely high viscosity so that it often resembles a paste rather than a liquid.

Pumping for Crude

Procedure

1. Copy the Oil Viscosity Data Table on a sheet of paper.

2. Fill the plastic bottle to the halfway mark with gravel.

3. Pour 100 ml vegetable oil into the plastic bottle. (Use the graduated cylinder to measure it.)

4. Put the plastic spray pump back on the bottle, making sure that you work the spray tube down into the gravel as far as possible.

5. Attach one end of the plastic tube to the spray pump, and place the other end in the graduated cylinder.

6. Squeeze the pump until no more oil comes from the gravel. Observe the amount of oil you collected in the cylinder and record the figure in the recovered-oil column of the Oil Viscosity Data Table.

Oil Viscosity Data Table	
Method	Recovered Oil (ml)
Oil	
Oil and Cold Water	
Oil and Hot Water	
Oil, Hot Water, and Detergent	

7. Dispose of the oil in the graduated cylinder and add 50 ml of cold water to the spray bottle. Repeat step #6. Allow the oil to settle on top of the water in the cylinder before measuring the amount of oil you recovered and recording it in the data table.

8. Dispose of the oil and add 50 ml of hot water to the spray bottle. Repeat step #6 and record your result.

9. Dispose of the oil and add 8 drops of dishwashing liquid to the spray bottle. Repeat step #6. This time, you have a wait a little while before the oil separates and you can record your result.

Result

The least amount of oil was recovered from the first procedure. Slightly more oil was recovered by adding the cold water, and con-siderably more was recovered by adding the hot water. But the most dramatic result occurred after you added the dishwashing liquid.

Explanation

The first procedure was the least successful because nothing altered the naturally high viscosity of the oil as it clung to the gravel and to the bottom of the spray bottle. Adding cold water to the oil improved the result somewhat. Oil is lighter than water, so it floats on the surface of water and is easier to reach with the pump. Hot water lowers the viscosity of oil so that more of it can be pumped with less effort. And finally, adding dishwashing liquid to the oil emulsifies it so that it combines with the water, giving it the lowest viscosity possible.

Five Types of Fossilization

You Will Need

- Modeling clay
- Plaster of paris
- Sand
- Epsom salt
- Small drinking glass
- Seashells
- Leaf samples
- Drawing pad
- Disposable pie pan
- Bucket and stirrer
- #2 lead pencil (not sharp)
- Tweezers
- Teaspoon
- Tape What kind??
- Yarn
- Aluminum foil
- Toothpick
- Warm water

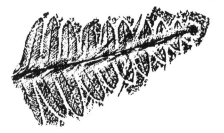

Fossils come in many different varieties. Each type of fossil is the result of a different fossilization process, and each tells paleontologists—scientists who study fossils—something unique about the material preserved. In this project you will replicate five different types of fossilization and learn why each is important.

Procedure

1. Flatten the modeling clay into a thick pancake.

2. Take one of the seashells and press it firmly into the clay. Carefully remove the shell from the clay.

3. Mix some plaster and water in the paper cup until it has the consistency of paste. Spoon the plaster into the clay mold you just made and immediately wash off the spoon.

4. Mix another batch of plaster in the bucket and add a ½ cup (120 ml) of sand. You should have just enough plaster to fill the pie pan.

5. Pour the plaster into the pie pan and carefully press your hand into the plaster. Allow the plaster to dry.

6. Pour warm water into the small glass to about the halfway mark. Spoon in Epsom salt and stir. Continue adding salt and stirring until no more salt will dissolve in the water.

7. Take a piece of yarn and wad it up into a ball. Drop the ball into the Epsom salt solution and leave it there for 1 minute. Use the tweezers to remove the yarn and place it on a piece of aluminum foil to dry.

8. Turn your leaf samples so that the venous sides (revealing the veins) face you. Attach them to a sheet of drawing paper with a little tape at the stem. Place a second piece of paper over the leaf samples.

9. Use broad, firm strokes of the #2 pencil to darken the area directly above each leaf sample.

10. Carefully peel the modeling clay from the hardened plaster so that you preserve the clay mold. Use a toothpick to scrape off any bits of clay that remain stuck to the plaster cast.

11. Turn the aluminum pie pan upside down and gently tap it to remove the cast of your hand.

12. Place all of your objects in a row in this order: seashell, yarn, leaf rubbings, clay mold, and plaster handprint.

Explanation

The seashell represents what paleontologists call original remains. These are fossils that do not change when an animal dies. Besides shells, the remains can include teeth and bones. But if conditions are right, the softer parts of an animal's body may be preserved, too. Tar, quicksand, bogs, and even glacial ice can preserve animal flesh for thousands of years. Delicate insects have been preserved in amber, the hardened and gemlike state of tree sap.

The yarn represents replaced remains. These fossils consist of animal or plant matter that has been mineralized. The minerals—such as calcite, quartz, and pyrite—are carried by groundwater and seep into organic tissue, gradually replacing it. But the mineral replacement copies the original material very closely, as anyone who has even seen a petrified tree knows.

The leaf rubbings imitate delicate carbonized remains that paleontologists sometimes find in hard shale. These remains are exact copies of the organisms, and their details can tell scientists much about the ancient plant world. A carbonized fossil is formed when a leaf or other delicate plant structure is buried in mud. While the mud turns to shale, the leaf changes chemically until only the carbon is left, leaving a thin film on the shale.

The clay mold illustrates the mold, imprint, and cast fossil. This type of fossilization occurs when animal or plant material is buried in mud. The mud turns into hard shale, and eventually the organic material dissolves, leaving a mold behind. If the shale develops small cracks, mineral-laden groundwater seeps into the mold and creates a detailed cast of the dissolved material. Many ocean fossils, such as the trilobite, are preserved this way.

The handprint represents what paleontologists call trace fossils. These are imprints in sedimentary rock that you imitated by adding sand to the plaster. The footprints of dinosaurs are trace fossils. So are wormholes and other burrows of insects in soft rock. Trace fossils are different from other fossils because they tell paleontologists about the activity of an animal while it was still alive.

Echolocate the Ocean Floor

Geologists use sound to study the shapes of things they can't directly observe. When a sound wave travels to a distant object, it bounces off the object and returns to its source. This technique, called echolocation, is similar to what a bat does naturally to find its way around in the dark. But do you think echolocation would help describe a very large object like the ocean floor? This project uses a series of bell rings to simulate the transformation of echolocation data into graphical data.

Listening for Pings

Procedure

1. Sit opposite your friend at the small table. The table represents the navigation room of a ship sent to map an unknown portion of the ocean floor.

2. Decide who will ring the bell and who will record result. The bell ringer represents the echolocation device.

3. The bell ringer sends ping #1 to the ocean floor. Using the clock, the recorder must mark in seconds how long it takes the ping to echo back. The second ping of the bell represents the echo.

4. The bell ringer sends out ping #2, and the recorder must again count the seconds between this ping and its echo.

5. Proceed for eight more pairs of pings, each time recording the time interval between ping and echo.

The Echo Equation

Procedure

1. Use each of the recorded time intervals in the equation below. The equation represents the time it takes for the ping to reach the ocean floor, multiplied by the speed of sound in water (1,500 meters per second).

$$\text{Number of Seconds} \times 2 \times \frac{\text{Speed of Sound}}{\text{in Water}} = \text{Ocean Depth}$$

For example, if 4 seconds elapsed between ping #1 and its echo, then it took 2 seconds for the ping to reach the ocean floor.

$$2 \text{ Seconds} \times 1,000 \text{ meters per second} = 2,000 \text{ meters}$$

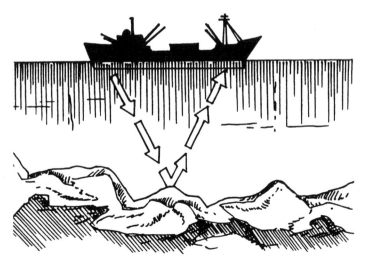

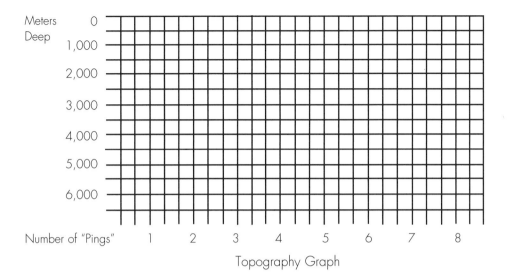

Topography Graph

2. Continue to translate each of your time intervals into meters until you reach the eighth and last ping.

Making the Picture

Procedure

1. Copy the topography chart on a piece of graph paper. Draw a dot at the meter depth that corresponds to each of the pings. Remember, each ping is actually a pair of pings, one representing the echo.

2. Connect the dots on the graph paper.

Result

A line with peaks and valley emerges. This line represents the transformation of your time-interval data into meters-deep data.

Explanation

By connecting the dots, you've transformed numerical information into a graphic depiction of an imaginary ocean floor. The topography of the ocean floor was determined entirely by the intervals between each ping and its echo. In fact, the bell ringer can create any landscape he chooses by varying these interval times.

Did You Know?

Geologists and oceanographers aren't the only scientists to use echolocation. Both Russian and American astronomers used this technique to reveal details about the cloud-hidden surface of Venus. Even archaeologists find echolocation useful in determining the shapes and designs of buried structures before they undertake the risky process of excavation.

Sparks & Waves

Electrostatic Water Generator

Proto-Battery: The Voltaic Pile

Magnetic Fields Surrounding a Conductor

A Macroscopic View of Magnetic Domains

Create a Leyden Jar Capacitor

Disc Electrophorus

Radio-Wave Emissions from Your Computer

A Dancing Spring in Electrolyte Solution

Compare Thermal Conduction in Four Metals

Electrical Energy from a Thermopile

Observe Eddy-Current Magnetic Attraction

The Curie Point of Gadolinium

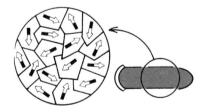

Electrostatic Water Generator

You Will Need

- 3 plastic buckets (1 disposable)
- 6 large Styrofoam cups, same size
- 2 pipette nozzles with regulator valves (*medical or science supply store*)
- Stepladder
- Push-broom handle
- T-attachment pipe (*hardware store*)
- Narrow 5-foot (1.5-m) rubber tubing
- 2 unpainted wire hangers
- 2 bricks
- Wire cutters
- Drill
- Silicone caulking
- Scissors

This project uses ordinary water to demonstrate how high-voltage static electricity can be created through the action of air against a falling water droplet.

Procedure

1. Use the wire cutters to cut the hooks from the hangers; then bend each hanger into the shape shown in the drawing (right). Make sure the loop at the end of each hanger is no more than 1 cm (0.4 inch).

2. Bend one end of each hanger into an L-

Hanger, Brick, and Bucket Assembly

shape, and place this end under a brick.

3. Position two buckets on the Styrofoam cups so that the rims of the buckets are no more than 5 cm (2 inches) apart. Each bucket should have three cups supporting it.

4. Push the pipette nozzles into the T-attachment pipe so that they point down, using a length of rubber tubing if necessary. Connect more rubber tubing to the T-attachment, leaving one end of the tubing free to connect with the third bucket.

5. Tape the pipettes and T-attachment onto the push-broom stick. Straddle the push-broom stick between the middle rungs of the stepladder and tape the stick in place. Position the ladder over the two buckets so that each nozzle is directly over a bucket.

6. Place the weighted ends of the hanger wires into the bucket, and carefully position the wires so that they cross and the loop of each wire sits directly below the nozzle of the opposite bucket (see drawing). There should be no more than 1 cm (0.4 inch) of space separating the wires where they cross.

7. Drill a hole in the side wall of the third bucket near the bottom. Push the end of the T-attachment tubing through the hole and seal around the tubing with silicon caulking.

8. Place the bucket with attached tubing on the top rung of the stepladder, and fill the bucket with water.

9. Open one nozzle and adjust the trickle of water so that the trickle breaks into droplets just at the point where the water passes through the hanger loop. After about a minute, open the second nozzle and make the same adjustment.

Result

After about 2 minutes of dual-nozzle dripping, droplets from both nozzles avoid falling straight down into their buckets. Instead, droplets veer, jump, and bend toward the farther bucket. As the process continues, droplets appear to float and fan out in all directions. A sudden electrical spark between the two wires restores neutrality, but as the droplets continue to fall, the entire process repeats.

Successful operation of this project may take some patient adjusting. If nothing happens after 2 minutes, check to make sure the hangers are no more than 1 cm (0.4 inches) apart where they cross. Also make sure that the water droplets fall through the loops. With a little adjusting of the apparatus and the right amount of dryness in the air, you'll be rewarded with a spectacular result.

Explanation

Protons and electrons (positive and negative charges) exist in roughly equal amounts in all substances. This means that most things are electrically neutral. You can easily upset this balance by rubbing one object against another—wool against plastic, tissue against a comb, or your feet against a carpet. The electrostatic generator uses the friction of air against droplets to separate the negative and positive charges in ordinary water.

When you opened the first nozzle, water droplets fell through the loop, losing electrons. These electrons were carried through the wire into the water of bucket #2. The droplets, stripped of electrons and now positively charged, continued falling into bucket #1. So after a minute of dripping, you have negatively charged water in bucket #2 and positively charged water in bucket #1. (The Styrofoam cups act as insulators and keep the buckets from discharging into the ground.)

When you opened the second nozzle, the droplets resisted falling straight down because of the strong negative charge of the water directly below them. (Remember, like charges repel each other.) The same situation existed for the droplets of the first nozzle; each falling droplet is repelled by the strong positive charge of the bucket below.

So what happens? Eventually, most of the droplets stop falling straight down and head for the bucket with the opposite (attracting) charge. Or some droplets continue falling but split in half. Soon droplets appear to fan and float in all directions, continually increasing the charges in the buckets. Eventually the static electricity builds to a level where it discharges in a spark at the crossing point of the two wires. This spark restores electrical neutrality for a while, but soon the process repeats and accelerates into a second discharge.

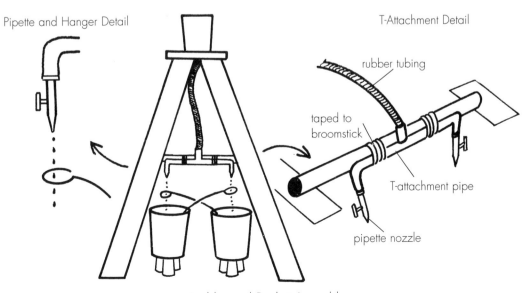

Pipette and Hanger Detail

T-Attachment Detail

rubber tubing

taped to broomstick

T-attachment pipe

pipette nozzle

Ladder and Bucket Assembly

Proto-Battery: The Voltaic Pile

While dissecting a frog one day in 1780, the Italian physician Luigi Galvani noticed that the dead frog's legs would twitch when he touched them with his copper and iron dissecting knives at the same time. He showed the trick to his friend Alessandro Volta, who correctly assumed that the twitching was due to electrical energy generated by two different metals separated by something moist. Soon Volta was off building pancake-shaped piles of different metals, separated by cloth soaked in dilute acetic acid or brine. This *voltaic pile*, as it came to be known, produced a steady stream of electrical current whenever it was needed. It was the first battery. In this project you'll make a miniature model of Volta's great invention.

Procedure

1. Fold the paper towels into 19 squares, each square about the size of a postage stamp.

2. Make a stack of coins by alternating pennies and dimes, but place a square of paper towel between each coin.

3. Lay the stack on its side in the plate, and carefully wrap the rubber band around the stack to hold it together.

4. Tuck one of the galvanometer's wires under the rubber band at one end of the pile, and tuck the other wire at the opposite end of the pile. Observe the galvanometer needle.

5. Carefully pour the lemon juice over the pile, making sure that the juice soaks the pieces of towel between the coins. Observe the galvanometer again.

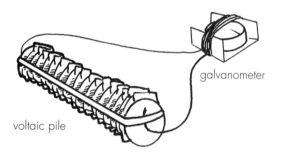

Testing Electrical Current from a Voltaic Pile

Result

The needle of the galvanometer didn't move when you attached the wires to the dry stack of coins. But when you added the lemon juice, the needle turned nearly 90 degrees from its axis, indicating that a current of electricity was flowing through the pile.

CAUTION: To avoid getting shocked, don't touch the wet ends of the pile with your fingers. Disconnect the galvanometer by holding the insulated parts of the wires and tugging until the stripped ends pull out from under the rubber band. Allow the pile to dry before taking it apart.

Explanation

Unlike static electricity, which exists in a field around a charged object, electrical current flows through a conducting material. When we separate two different metals (the electrodes of a battery) by a conducting liquid like lemon juice (the electrolyte), the juice reacts with the more electrically active metal and causes electrons (or electricity) to flow away from it into the less active metal.

You can think of electrical current as water moving from a higher place to a lower place. In this case, the electricity flowed from the copper coin to the non-copper coin and continued flowing right through the entire length of the pile.

Did You Know?

The modern flashlight battery is very similar in design to the voltaic pile. But instead of coins, zinc is placed around a carbon rod at the battery's center, and the electrolyte is a much more active combination of ammonia and zinc chloride.

Magnetic Fields
Surrounding a Conductor

You Will Need

- Wire coat hanger or 2-foot (60-cm) stiff wire
- 2 pieces insulated (plastic-coated) copper wire
- 2 D-cell batteries
- Masking tape
- Cardboard
- Iron filings
- Teaspoon or 5-ml spoon
- Scissors
- Pliers

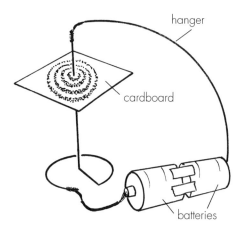

Battery, Cardboard, and Hanger Assembly

This project proves that a magnetic field or magnetic envelope surrounds a current-carrying conductor at all times. The magnetic field has a characteristic shape that will reveal itself with the help of iron filings.

Procedure

1. Use the pliers to bend the coat hanger or thick wire into the shape shown in the illustration.

2. Poke the straight end of the coat hanger through the cardboard's center, and push the cardboard down along the wire a few inches.

3. Use the scissors to carefully strip off about ½ inch (1.25 cm) of plastic insulation from both ends of each piece of wire.

4. Tape the two D-cell batteries together, making sure that the positive end of one battery touches the negative end of the other.

5. Tape the stripped ends of wire to the ends of your batteries.

6. Connect, by twisting or taping, one of the wires to the bottom of the hanger stand. Leave the other wire unattached for now.

7. Carefully sprinkle 1 teaspoon (5 ml) of iron filings around the wire. Sprinkle them so that they evenly coat the cardboard.

8. Connect the unattached battery wire to the top of the wire stand.

9. Gently tap the cardboard a few times and observe what happens to the iron filings.

Result

With a few taps, the iron filings will form into a series of concentric circles with the wire at their center. Disconnect the top wire, tap the cardboard, and the circles disappear. Reconnect the wire and the circles reappear. Clearly, the arrangement of the circles reflects the presence of electrical current moving through the hanger.

Explanation

From the arrangement of the circles, we can see that the magnetic fields exist in concentric tubes or envelopes that expand from the surface of the wire hanger. These envelopes only show the presence, not the direction, of the current. If we were to reverse the wires on the hanger so that the current flowed in the opposite direction, the circles would look the same. Although scientists have worked hard to design wires that minimize electro-magnetic fields, this phenomenon exists around virtually every wire you see, indoors or out.

A Macroscopic View of Magnetic Domains

You Will Need

- Test tube with stopper or clear toothbrush case
- Bar magnet
- Small compass
- Iron filings

Through the study of atomic physics, scientists now know much more about magnetism, especially how it occurs on the molecular level. A breakthrough in magnetic theory was the concept of magnetic domains, which exist in all magnetic material. A *magnetic domain* is a molecular "neighborhood" where all the molecules point in the same direction. You can think of a magnetic domain as a tiny magnet that exists inside materials that are either magnets themselves or are attracted to magnets. For example, an ordinary iron nail, while not a magnet, still contains billions of magnetic domains.

So why isn't the iron nail a magnet? Because each magnetic domain points in a different direction, and only with a little coaxing from the outside will they line up and combine their magnets into one large magnet. This arrangement is only tempo-rary, however, since the domains can easily fall out of alignment again. In this project, you will test the theory of magnetic domains by using a "solid" iron object made from iron filings.

Procedure

1. Fill the test tube or toothbrush case about halfway with iron filings.

2. Bring the bottom end of the tube near a compass; then bring the upper end near the compass. Record you observations.

3. Slowly stroke the test tube in a downward direction 20 times with one end of the bar magnet.

4. Repeat step #2.

5. Shake the test tube vigorously.

6. Repeat step #2.

Result

The first time you held the compass to the test tube, either end of the needle was slightly attracted and shifted toward the iron filings. After you stroked the test tube 20 times, the north-seeking needle of the compass was strongly attracted to one end of the tube while the south-seeking needle was repelled. This effect was reversed when you held the compass to the other end of the test tube. After shaking the test tube, the original result repeated.

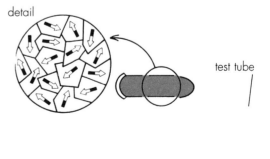

detail

test tube

Unmagnetized Atoms

Explanation

Think of each piece of iron filing as a molecule. As you stroked the test tube, its "molecules" all began to line up in the same direction so that the tube itself became a magnet with a distinct north and south pole. This was proven with the compass test.

When you shook the test tube, the alignment of the molecules was destroyed and they returned to their original random positions. This returned the test tube to its demagnetized state.

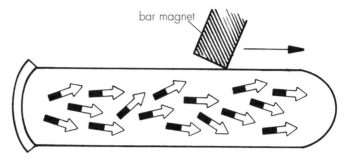

bar magnet

Test Tube Stroked with the Pole of a Bar Magnet

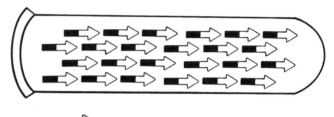

magnetized atom

Test Tube with Magnetized Atoms

Create a Leyden Jar Capacitor

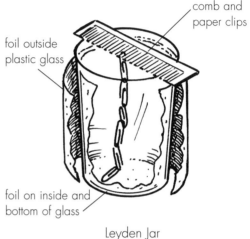

comb and paper clips

foil outside plastic glass

foil on inside and bottom of glass

Leyden Jar

You Will Need

- Thin plastic disposable glass
- Aluminum foil
- Spray adhesive
- Plastic comb
- 10 unpainted paper clips
- Insulated (plastic-coated) wire
- Teaspoon or 5-ml spoon
- Scissors
- Electrophorus (see "Disc Electrophorus")

The first Leyden jar was built by Dutch mathematician and scientist Pieter van Musschenbroek at the University of Leyden in Holland. Although the phenomenon of static electricity had been observed and studied, many scientists struggled to find a way to put this mysterious force to work. The solution would involve finding a way to store, save, and accumulate the short, intense electrical discharges that were relatively easy to produce. In designing the Leyden jar, van Musschenbroek effectively invented the first electrical-charge storage device, or capacitor.

Building the Leyden Jar

Procedure

1. Spray the outside bottom and outside walls of the plastic glass with adhesive, leaving only about a quarter of the glass unsprayed near the rim.
2. Wrap a single sheet of aluminum foil around the glass at the sprayed surfaces. Use the back of a teaspoon to burnish the foil so that it adheres very closely to the surface of the glass.
3. Spray the inside bottom and inside walls of the glass with the adhesive and apply aluminum foil, burnishing it as before.
4. Make a chain out of the paper clips by linking them together. Make sure that your chain is long enough so that the bottom paper clip lies flat against the bottom of the glass.
5. Push the top paper clip into the teeth of a plastic comb so that part of the clip sticks up from the comb and can act as a terminal.

Charging the Leyden Jar

Procedure

1. Use scissors to strip the ends of a piece of insulated wire.
2. Charge the electrophorus following the procedure described in "A Macroscopic View of Magnetic Domains."
3. Bring the surface of the electrophorus close to the protruding paper clip of the Leyden jar. A spark will jump from the electrophorus to the clip.

4. Repeat this procedure ten times; then use a little tape to attach one stripped end of the insulated wire to the outer aluminum foil of the glass.

CAUTION: Do not touch the foil and the exposed paper clip at the same time.

---

5. Carefully bring the other stripped end of the wire close to the protruding paper clip and watch what happens.

Result

A blue spark jumps from the wire to the paper clip. This spark will be many times stronger than the sparks your electrophorus produced.

Explanation

Every time the electrophorus discharged into the Leyden jar, the jar stored the charge. After ten charges, the jar contained a considerable amount of electrical energy. You discharged this energy at once by touching the stripped wire to the protruding clip.

The Leyden jar can also be discharged in your body if you touch the stripped end of wire and paper clip at the same time. But Leyden jars are powerful containers of energy, and you could get quite a surprising shock.

The success of your Leyden jar depends to a great extent on the quality of your glass. If the plastic glass yields a disappointing result, try using a small glass scientific beaker. This type of "hard glass" will optimize the result.

Did You Know?

People sometimes confuse the workings of a Leyden-jar capacitor with those of a voltaic cell, or battery. Although they are similar in some ways, a capacitor and battery function very differently. Whereas a Leyden jar stores electricity as a pail might contain water, a battery is a more dynamic system that creates electrical current by separating two different metals of different conductivities with a conducting liquid (electrolyte). The electrolyte reacts more strongly with the more conductive metal and allows electrons to flow from it into the less conductive metal, somewhat like water moving from a high place to a lower place. The difference between the electrical potentials of the two metals is called voltage.

Disc Electrophorus

You Will Need

- Old vinyl phonograph record
- Wool sweater or shirt
- Metal lid from a screw-top jar
- ½-inch × 12-inch (1.25 × 30-cm) wooden dowel
- Fine-gauge sandpaper
- Carpenter's glue

Vinyl Record for Testing Electrophorus

The electrophorus was invented by Alessandro Volta in 1775. He was looking for a simple device to carry successive charges of static electricity into a Leyden jar for storage (see "Create a Leyden Jar Capacitor"). This design is uncomplicated and can be varied as long as you understand the underlying basics of how an electrophorus works.

Procedure

1. Remove the cardboard backing from the lid of a screw-top jar, then sand the front of the lid to remove any paint. Rinse the lid in water to wash away the sanded paint particles. Allow the lid to dry.

2. Use some glue to attach one end of the wooden dowel to the back of the lid. Make sure the dowel is comfortable to hold and keeps your hand from touching the lid. Allow the glue to dry.

3. When you're ready to use the electrophorus, rub the vinyl phonograph record with the woolen material for about 30 seconds. Pick up the electrophorus by the handle and lay the disc on the surface of the record. Touch the disc with the finger of your other hand for just a second (this provides a ground for the charge).

4. Carefully lift the disc by the handle and bring it close to a knuckle of your other hand. Observe what happens.

5. Repeat step #3 and bring the electrophorus close to a doorknob. Observe the result.

Result

A blue spark jumps first from the surface of the lid to your knuckle, and then from the lid to the doorknob. Depending on the size of the electrophorus and the dryness of the air, this spark can be close to 6,000 volts.

Explanation

Under normal circumstances, an object has the same number of negatively charged electrons and positively charged protons. This means that the object is electrically neutral. However, electrons can move about freely while protons remain more stationary.

An electrophorus works by allowing positively charged protons to stick to its surface while simultaneously letting the negatively charged electrons flow away. This turns the surface of the electrophorus into a container for positively charged protons and gives it a strong positive charge. This charge is dispelled in a spark when the electrophorus is brought close to a neutral material again.

When you rubbed the record with the wool, you gave the record a strong negative charge. But because the surface of the record is grooved rather than flat, the flowing electrons concentrate closer to the record's true surface—that is, between the grooves rather than at their tips. The leftover protons remain at the tips of the grooves where the electrophorus makes contact with them.

Touching your finger to the electrophorus while it rests on the record allows whatever stray electrons that remain on the electrophorus and record to flow through your body and into the ground. This leaves only protons in the electrophorus now so that it has a strong positive charge.

Radio-Wave Emissions from Your Computer

You Will Need

- Computer
- AM/FM portable radio

If you look at the label on the central-processing unit of your computer (the tower of a PC or the monitor base of a Macintosh), you'll see a sticker indicating that your computer complies with all FCC regulations for radio-wave emissions. It might seem strange to think of a computer emitting radio waves, but computers do just that, as this project will show you.

Procedure

1. Set the portable radio on an AM station and turn the dial until you hear the soft static between stations.

2. Turn on the computer, and listen for any change in the static.

3. Gradually move the radio toward the processing unit. Record the distance at which the static becomes very pronounced and leave the radio there.

4. Place a floppy disc in your computer and listen for any changes in the static.

5. Turn off the monitor, but leave the hard drive running and listen for changes in static.

6. Shut down the hard drive and leave the monitor on and listen for changes in static.

7. Find the processor speed of your computer (it's written on the back label) and switch your radio to FM.

8. Tune the radio to the same speed as your processor. For example, if your computer processor speed is 100 megahertz (MHz), tune the dial to 100, and repeat steps #2–6.

9. From the information you gathered, try to determine on which band—AM or FM—the static was more pronounced.

Result

Although both AM and FM pick up radio-wave interference from your computer, the interference is much more pronounced on the AM band. This band also detected interference farther away than the FM band. (Radio waves travel differently on FM and resist interference.) On both AM and FM, the static grew louder when the computer was forced to do some work, like recognize a floppy disc. Switching off the processor while keeping the monitor on decreased the static noticeably, while switching the monitor off while keeping the processor on decreased the static only minimally.

Explanation

The radio waves emanating from your computer are simply another form of electromagnetic energy. This is why many devices that have nothing directly to do with communication will still emit radio waves that can interfere with communication devices. For this reason, the pilots of commercial flights will always ask passengers to turn off their laptop computers during the takeoff and landing, when radio communication with the control tower is essential.

A Dancing Spring in Electrolyte Solution

You Will Need

- Thin copper wire
- Thick copper wire or copper nail
- 2 pieces insulated (plastic-coated) wire
- Small cork or Styrofoam ball
- Small bowl
- Sharp pencil
- Salt
- 6-volt battery
- Stack of books
- Tape
- Scissors

This project describes electrical conductivity, magnetism, and something new—the properties of a liquid conductor called an *electrolyte*.

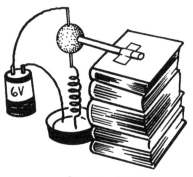

Dancing Spring

Procedure

1. To make the spring, twist the thin copper wire around the pencil in a coil. Keep the twists close together but avoid overlapping the wire. Carefully slip the wire from the pencil and test your spring's elasticity. If the spring is too tightly coiled, start again, making the twists farther apart.

2. Carefully push the thick copper wire through the cork or Styrofoam ball so that the wire sticks out at both ends. Push the sharp end of the pencil into the side of the ball.

3. Stack some books, and tape the eraser end of the pencil to the top of the stack. The tip of the copper wire should overhang the book by about 6 inches (15 cm).

4. Straighten out each end of your spring and twist one of the ends around the thick copper wire sticking out from the ball.

5. Using the scissors, strip the plastic insulation from the ends of both pieces of insulated wire. Attach each wire to a different terminal of the battery.

6. Attach the opposite end of one of the wires to the thick copper wire sticking out of the ball.

7. Fill the small bowl with warm water, and add salt until no more salt dissolves. Place the end of the copper spring in the saltwater so that the wire sits just below the water's surface.

8. Take the disconnected piece of insulated wire from the battery, and gently dip the stripped end into the saltwater.

Result

When you touch the end of wire to the saltwater, the spring jumps around in the water, alternately coiling and uncoiling.

Explanation

When a substance like salt dissolves in water, it releases charged particles called ions that move that about freely and behave very much like the metallic bonds of metals. Freely moving particles allow electrical energy to pass through, and so saltwater, as well as acidic solutions like vinegar and lemon juice, become liquid conductors of electricity, or electrolytes.

With the saltwater as an electrolyte, the battery, wires, and copper spring make a complete electrical circuit. When you touch the end of the battery-connected wire to the saltwater, you complete the circuit so that electricity travels in a continuous loop. Electrical current passing through the spring turns it into a magnet with a north and a south pole. The creation of magnetism from electricity or electricity from magnetism is called *induction.*

Since north and south poles attract each other, the spring pulls together. But when this happens, the end of the spring pops out of the water, breaking the circuit and stopping the flow of electricity. With no electricity, the spring no longer behaves like a magnet and stretches out so that the end once again dips into the saltwater. This restores the electrical circuit so that the spring becomes a magnet again and the bouncing continues.

Compare Thermal Conduction in Four Metals

You Will Need

- Copper, iron, brass, and aluminum strips, all the same size and thickness
- 4 bricks, same size
- Candle
- Sheet metal clippers
- Stopwatch or clock with a second hand

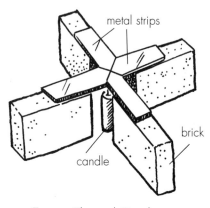

Testing Thermal Conduction

Not only do various metals demonstrate different electrical and magnetic properties, but how efficiently a metal conducts heat can also reveal much about its molecular structure. This project compares the thermal conductivity of four metals—copper, iron, brass, and aluminum.

Procedure

1. Use the sheet-metal clippers to carefully clip one end of each metal strip into a point.

2. Light the candle and allow a little molten wax to pool near the flame. Then carefully tip the candle so that no more than one drop of wax spills onto the square end of each metal strip. If more than one drop spills, wait until the wax dries and then scrape the extra drops off with your fingernail. Each wax drop represents about 1 milliliter of material.

3. Place 4 bricks together (see illustration). Place the metal strips on top of the bricks so that their pointed ends meet.

4. Put the candle under the point where the metal strips join. The candle's wick should be about ½ inch (1.25 cm) below the metal.

5. Carefully light the candle, start the stopwatch, and observe the wax droplet on each strip. When each drop liquefies, record the time.

Result

The best thermal conductor of the four metals will melt the drop first. Record the time interval of each melting and deduct which of the four metals has the best thermal conductivity. Although you should do your own experimentation, we rated conductivity from best to worst as follows: (1) copper, (2) aluminum, (3) brass, (4) iron.

Explanation

Conductivity, whether electrical or thermal, depends on the atomic structure of a material. Good conductors are composed of atoms with freely moving electrons. This means that the atom's electrons do not remain in fixed orbits around the atom's nucleus. Instead they move in a more "fluid" state that allows electrical (or thermal) energy to pass through. Still, a strong attachment, called a metallic bond, exists between these electrons and their nuclei. Nonconducting materials such as wood and glass are held together by covalent bonds. Electrons in these substances are attached to the nuclei or atoms in a fixed position and can't move about freely. You can visualize a metallic bond as a kind of bead curtain and a covalent bond as a chain-link fence.

As a result of heat absorption, the molecules of the various metals receive increased energy that increases their speed. Different metals require different amounts of heat in order to reach the same degree of internal energy or molecular motion. The ratio of the amount of heat required to raise the temperature of a substance by one unit to the amount of heat required to raise the temperature of an equal mass of a different substance (usually water) by the same amount is known as specific heat.

Electrical Energy from a Thermopile

To measure the electromagnetic output of your thermopile, you first have to construct a simple device called a galvanometer. A galvanometer senses electrical current by the motion of a needle. This is why a compass is a good starting point.

Constructing a Compass Galvanometer

Procedure

1. Cut the cardboard sheet into a rectangle, as wide as the compass but long enough to fold up around it on opposite sides.
2. Place the compass inside this cradle, making sure that the needle points to the folded edge of cardboard.
3. Wrap 3 feet (90 cm) of copper wire around the cradle and compass so that you have about a foot of free wire sticking out on each side of the compass. To make your galvanometer easy to read, wrap the copper wire around the north-south orientation of the needle.

4. Use the scissors to strip about 1 inch (2.5 cm) of plastic insulation from the ends of the wire. Use these stripped ends of wire to connect your galvanometer to any device.

The Thermopile

Procedure

1. Twist a piece of iron wire with a piece of copper wire so that you have one coiled wire.
2. Repeat this procedure for the remaining pieces of iron and copper wires so that you wind up with four twisted wires.
3. Twist all four twisted wires together so that you have a thick piece of wire consisting of four iron wires and four copper wires. This is the conducting coil of your thermopile.
4. Bend the coil to form seven junctions (see illustration).
5. Place the coil flat and tape each free end of the thermopile to a wire on the galvanometer.
6. Hold the hair dryer about 4 inches (10 cm) from the thermopile and observe the movement of the needle in the galvanometer.

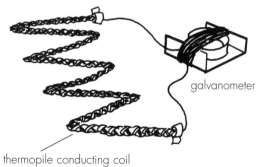

galvanometer

thermopile conducting coil

Thermopile and Galvonometer

Result

As the coil heats, the compass needle moves farther from its initial north-south orientation, indicating an electric current is being produced by the action of the heat upon the coil.

Explanation

Certain metals, when placed together, have the ability to turn radiating heat—that is, heat that travels in waves through the air—into electrical energy. Scientists call these metallic combinations thermoelectric couples. Copper and iron make up one of these couples; so do bismuth and antimony.

Observe Eddy-Current Magnetic Attraction

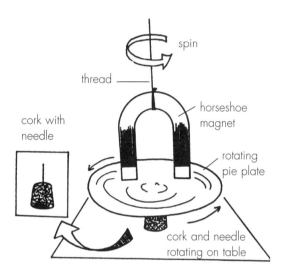

Eddy-Current Apparatus

You Will Need

- Large horseshoe magnet
- Small aluminum-foil pie plate
- Sewing needle
- Cork or small piece of Styrofoam
- 1-foot (30-cm) thread
- Stack of books
- Ruler
- Tape

Many familiar devices wouldn't be possible without magnets. But is a magnet's attractive power its only useful feature, or could it be that what a magnet doesn't attract can be equally important? This project explores weak magnetic attraction. In creating a simple eddy-current motor, you'll begin to recognize a familiar device. To obtain the best result from this project, set it up in a place protected from drafts.

Procedure

1. Place the aluminum pie plate in the freezer overnight.

2. Push the sewing needle through the center of the cork or Styrofoam so that its point sticks up. Use a little tape around the edges of the cork or Styrofoam to anchor it to the tabletop.

3. Remove the plate from the freezer, turn it upside down, and balance it on the needle so that it can easily spin. Some pie plates have a small indentation at their centers. If you have one of those, place the needle there.

4. Tie one end of the string to the horseshoe magnet and tie the other end to the end of the ruler. Secure the string to the ruler with a little tape.

5. Stack some books and place the ruler on top to make sure that the suspended magnet hangs no more than ½ inch (1.25 cm) above the pie plate. Place a few more books on top of the ruler to secure it.

6. Twist the magnet about 100 times, winding up the string.

7. Release the magnet and observe what happens to the pie plate.

Result

The pie plate will begin to spin along with the magnet, but not quite as fast.

Explanation

Since a magnet only attracts iron, what can be happening here? Obviously, some slight magnetic force exists between the magnet and the aluminum. Scientists describe this type of attraction as paramagnetic, meaning the weaker attraction of a magnet to a nonferrous (not-containing-iron) material. Aluminum is a paramagnetic material. The interesting thing about paramagnetic materials is that when you cool them they behave more like magnetic materials. This is why you froze the aluminum overnight.

As the horseshoe magnet spins, it creates magnetic eddy currents above the aluminum pan. In turn, these currents produce a cyclonic magnetic field above the aluminum pan's surface, causing the pan to spin. The magnetic field revolves in the same direction as the spinning magnet, and the faster the magnet spins, the stronger the eddy currents will be. The result? The pan spins faster and faster, although it will never quite keep up with the magnet.

Did You Know?

A car's speedometer operates on the eddy-flow principle. As the car moves, a magnet rotates at a certain speed, depending on the speed of the car. (Engineers carefully work out this equation.) This rotating magnet exerts a force on a disc made from a paramagnetic metal, like aluminum. The disc contains the pointer of the speedometer, which moves against a scale, indicating the car's speed.

The Curie Point of Gadolinium

You Will Need

- 2 strong bar magnets, same size
- Small piece of gadolinium foil *(science-supply store)*
- 1-foot (30-cm) thread
- Stack of books
- Ruler
- Tape
- Hooded lamp with 100-watt bulb
- Thermometer
- Clock with second hand
- Portable table

This project demonstrates that the magnetic properties of a material can change under certain conditions. The metal gadolinium is one of these materials.

Procedure

1. Make two stacks of books the same height.

2. Tape a bar magnet to each stack so that about 1 inch (2.5 cm) of magnet overhangs each stack. Make sure that the positive end of one magnet overhangs the first stack of books while the negative end of the other magnet overhangs the second stack of books. Arrange the stacks of books so that the magnets are about 1 inch (2.5 cm) apart.

3. Set up the portable table and tape one end of the ruler to the tabletop. Make sure the other end of the ruler overhangs the table by about 2 inches (5 cm).

4. Cut a 1-inch (2.5-cm) square piece of gadolinium foil and attach it with as little tape as possible to one end of the thread. Attach the other end of the thread to the ruler.

5. Hold the gadolinium foil piece between the two ends of the bar magnets. The thread should be taut.

6. Carefully release the foil so that it's suspended in midair between the two magnets. You may have to adjust the position of your ruler and thread to make sure this happens.

7. Carefully place the thermometer against one of the bar magnets.

8. Position the hooded lamp so that the bulb is about 5 inches (12.5 cm) from the suspended foil.

9. Turn on the lamp and observe the foil. Mark the time on your clock and watch the thermometer.

Result

After a little time, the foil will suddenly slip away from the bar magnets. Record the time of the drop as well as the temperature on the thermometer.

Explanation

Heating the foil with the lamp caused the gadolinium to lose its magnetic properties. Gadolinium, a rare-earth metal, behaves like iron when exposed to a magnet at room temperature. But when gadolinium is heated, it loses its magnetic properties. Scientists call the temperature at which a magnetic material loses its magnetism its Curie point (after the 19th century French physicist Pierre Curie). The Curie point for gadolinium is recorded on your thermometer. It should be around 28° Celsius or Centigrade (82.4° Fahrenheit).

Different metals have different Curie points. For example, iron loses its magnetism at 800°C (1472°F), and nickel loses its magnetism at 350°C (662°F). In each case, heating the metal causes the atoms to become so excited that they break out of their magnetic alignment.

Knowing a metal's Curie point is important when designing complicated machines that use magnets, particularly machines that work in demanding physical environments.

Did You Know?

Although heating some materials can cancel their magnetic attractiveness, cooling other materials can enhance magnetic attractiveness (see "Observe Eddy-Current Magnetic Attraction"). Aluminum, for example, behaves more like iron when cooled. Some rare-earth metals, when super-cooled by liquid nitrogen, become superconductors of electromagnetic energy and have amazingly potent magnetic properties.

Converting Celsius to Fahrenheit & Vice Versa

To convert Celsius to Fahrenheit, multiply the Celsius temperature by 9, divide the product by 5, and add 32. Here's the formula:

$$(C \text{ degrees} \times 9/5) + 32 = F \text{ degrees}$$

$$28° \text{ Celsius} \times 9 = 252$$
$$252 \div 5 = 50.4$$
$$50.4 + 32 = 82.4° \text{ Fahrenheit}$$

To convert Fahrenheit to Celsius, subtract 32 from the Fahrenheit temperature, multiply the difference by 5, and divide the product by 9. Here's the formula:

$$(F \text{ degrees} - 32) \times 5/9 = C \text{ degrees}$$

$$82.4° \text{ Fahrenheit} - 32 = 50.4$$
$$50.4 \times 5 = 252$$
$$252 \div 9 = 28° \text{ Celsius}$$

Eye & Mind

Two Turntable Stroboscopes

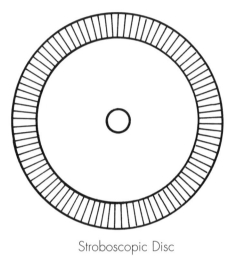

Stroboscopic Disc

You Will Need

- Phonograph with 78-rpm speed
- Phonograph record
- Electric lamp without shade
- White poster board
- White paper
- Compass
- Protractor
- Felt-tip marking pen
- Hole punch
- Scissors
- Ruler

Both the strobe light and stroboscope create the illusion of stopped motion. You can easily create a simple stroboscopic disc or stroboscopic strip that yields dramatic results on a phonograph turntable.

Stroboscopic Disc

Procedure

1. Use the compass to measure the diameter of the phonograph-record label, then draw a circle on the poster board with the same diameter. Draw a smaller circle inside the larger one so that you have a band about ½ inch (1.25 cm) thick.

2. Cut out the circle, and punch a hole in the center where the compass needle made a mark.

3. Use the marker to draw 92 equally spaced lines in the band of the circle. To do this, divide 360° (circumference of a circle) by 92 (degrees between each line) for the quotient 3.9. Round this off to 4 and use the

protractor to mark lines 4° apart on the edge of the circle. (Or enlarge the illustration above on a photocopier to a size that fits.)

4. Place the circle over the post of the turntable. Switch on the phonograph to a speed of 78 rpm.

5. Place the electric lamp near the spinning stroboscope. Record your observations.

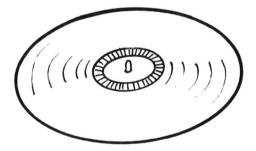

Phonograph Record with Stroboscopic Disc

Stroboscopic Strip

Procedure

1. Cut a strip of paper ½ × 5 inches (1.25 × 12.5 cm).

2. From one end of the paper, measure 4¾ inches (11.87 cm). Divide this into 92 equally spaced vertical lines. Each line will be about ¹⁄₁₆ inch (0.15 cm) long.

3. Loop the strip and connect the ends with a paper clip. Clip the lined portion of the clip over the blank portion so that the lines meet up accurately.

4. Place the strip over the label of the phonograph record, and switch on the phonograph to a speed of 78 rpm. Record your observations.

Result

As the turntable accelerates, the lines on both the disc and strip blur. However, when the turntable speed stabilizes at 78 rpm, the lines appear to stop.

Explanation

The apparent stopped motion of the lines indicates the frequency of the lightbulb. *Frequency* means the number of times anything takes place in a unit of time, in this case, a second. The current in a lightbulb reverses directions 60 times each second, which causes an imperceptible pulse in the apparent steady light of the bulb. Each reverse in direction is called a *cycle* and is measured in megahertz (MHz). So a 60 MHz lightbulb pulses at a rate of 3,600 times a second.

So why do the lines on the stroboscope appear to stop? Each time the light pulses on, the black lines in the stroboscope have turned exactly one space, giving the illusion that the disc hasn't moved at all!

You can figure out how many lines to draw on your stroboscopic disc by doing some simple arithmetic. If you want to see a strobe effect at 78 rpm, multiply 3,600 by 2 and divide by 78. This gives you the number 92.3, which you can round down to 92. If you mark 92 equally spaced lines on the disc, the lines will appear to stand still at 78 rpm.

$$3600 \times 2 \div 78 = 92.3 \text{ or } 92$$

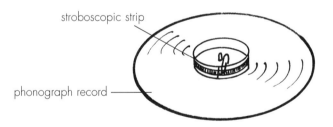

stroboscopic strip

phonograph record

Stroboscopic Strip around
Label of Phonograph Record

Stroboscopic Strip with 92 Lines

Rotating-Ring Illusion

You Will Need

- Phonograph
- Poster board
- 2 liter soft-drink bottle
- 30-inch (75-cm) brightly colored insulated (plastic-coated) wire
- Compass
- Ruler
- Hole punch
- Scissors
- Tape

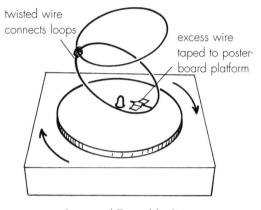

twisted wire connects loops

excess wire taped to poster-board platform

Ring and Turntable Setup

All simulated motion is based on the brain's inability to differentiate sequentially related visual elements when the elements are flashed or pulsed above a certain speed. This persistence of vision blends individual images together into one continuous image of motion. By manipulating the size and rotational speed of 3-D objects, you can create a similar effect. The rotating-ring illusion demonstrates this.

Procedure

1. Use the compass to draw a circle on the poster board 4½ inches (11.25 cm) in diameter. Cut out the circle and punch a hole at the circle's center where the compass needle made a mark.

2. Fill the 2-liter bottle with water to the very top. Place the cap on the bottle and screw it on tightly. You want the water to reinforce the bottle and keep its shape firm.

3. Cut the insulated wire into two pieces, each 15 inches (37.5 cm) long. Wrap a wire around the bottle and twist the 1-inch (2.5-cm) ends together tightly. Do the same for the second piece of wire.

4. Remove the wire hoops from the bottle. Connect the twisted wire of one hoop to the other hoop. Connect the twisted wire of the other hoop to the poster-board disc and tape it down securely.

5. Carefully bend the loops so that turntable, bottom loop, and top loop all sit at angles to one another.

6. Place the poster-board disc with attached loops over the post of the phonograph turntable.

7. Switch the phonograph to 33 rpm, then to 78 rpm (rpm = revolutions per minute). Observe the motion of the hoops.

Result

The wire hoops appear to disconnect and to tilt and rotate around each other's circumference. This effect is even more pronounced at 78 rpm.

Explanation

When two objects are placed at a certain distance relative to each other and rotated at a certain speed relative to their dimensions, the effect of virtual motion is created. Instead of seeing one object, all sections of which rotate at the same speed, you see two detached hoops rotating along each other's circumference.

Eye & Brain Perception of Motion

You Will Need

- Phonograph
- White poster board
- Compass
- Ruler
- Thick string
- Bold felt-tip marking pen
- Scissors
- Tape
- Poster of clouds
- Table

Cloud Poster and Turntable

This project demonstrates how eye and brain interpret motion together and what happens when that perceptual mechanism becomes fatigued.

Procedure

1. Use the ruler to measure the diameter of the phonograph turntable. Set the compass at this diameter and draw a circle on the poster board. Cut out the circle and punch a hole in the center of the circle where the compass needle made a mark.

2. Cut a piece of string with the same diameter as the circle.

3. Place the circle over the post of the turntable. Tie one end of the string to the post and tie the other end of the string to the middle of the felt-tip marking pen.

4. Hold the pen with the string taut, and carefully move the pen in a circle around the post so that it traces out a spiral on the circle. Remove the pen from the post.

5. Turn over the circle and repeat step #4, this time tracing a spiral in the opposite direction.

6. Tape the poster of clouds to the wall,

and place the phonograph on a table about 6 feet (1.8 m) from the poster.

7. Turn the phonograph to 78 rpm (or 33 rpm if your turntable doesn't have a 78-rpm setting) and stare at the spinning spiral for about 2 minutes.

8. Look up at the poster and stare at it.

9. Flip the circle to its other side and repeat steps #7 and 8.

Result

For about 10 seconds, the clouds in the poster appear to sweep across the sky in a direction opposite to that of the spiral.

Explanation

Receptors in the eyes work with the brain to detect inward and outward motion. When you look at stationary objects, inward and outward receptors are balanced. But when you look at a spiraling pattern, the motion makes one set of receptors tired. When you stop looking at the spiral and stare at the poster, the resting receptors take over. That's why you see motion in the opposite direction. This effect is most pronounced when objects have vague or complex outlines. That's why the clouds work so well. But trees and rock formations work just as well, and you can try substituting other pictures.

Virtual 3-D with a Polarized Lens

With the aid of a polarized lens from a pair of sunglasses, you can experience virtual 3-D motion superimposed over the simple swinging of a coin. You don't need to remove the lens from the sunglasses for the project to succeed.

Procedure

1. Bend and clip the coat hanger into an L-shape, and push the long side of the L into the Styrofoam base.

2. Use a little tape to attach the end of the thread to the back of a coin. Tie the other end of the thread to the top of the metal hanger.

3. Make sure your hanging coin assembly is in a well-lighted place, preferably with the light coming from the front rather than behind the object.

4. Sit directly in front of the assembly and pull the coin about 45 degrees from its resting position. Carefully release the coin so that it swings from side to side like a pendulum.

5. Hold the sunglasses sideways and hold one lens up to an eye. Observe the swinging motion of the coin with both eyes. Record your observations.

Result

The coin appears to travel in a loop around the wire it hangs from. The loop shrinks in size as the coin loses momentum.

Explanation

The simulation of three-dimensional motion over an essentially two-dimensional movement is the result of a time discrepancy between the two images that reach your brain. Because it allows only certain planes of light to pass through it, the polarized lens slows the light so that the image reaches this eye a fraction of a second slower than an image reaching the uncovered eye. This time displacement has the same effect as the spatial displacement of a stereoscopic photograph–it fools the eye and brain into seeing 3-D.

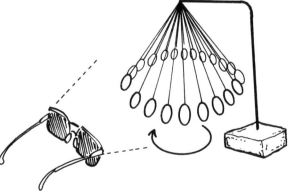

Polarized Glasses and Hanging Coins

Color Afterimage in the Retina

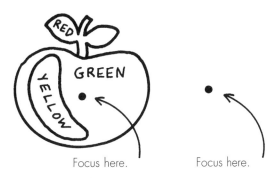

Focus here.   Focus here.

Straining our eyes, while never a good thing, can still result in some unusual and interesting effects. This project shows how the color receptor cells in your eyes, called cones, react to controlled fatigue.

Procedure

1. On a piece of white paper, copy the apple drawing using the indicated colors. Draw the apple on one side of the paper so that you leave a good amount of white space next to the drawing. Remember to include the two dots, one in the center of the apple and the other next to it in the blank area (about 2½ inches from the first dot).

2. Position the lamp over the drawing and stare at the apple, focusing on the dot inside. Do this for 1 minute. (Count or use a timer.) Try to lock your eyes to the dot, keeping your focus as steady as possible.

3. After the minute is up, lock your eyes on the dot on the blank side of the paper and wait about 10 seconds.

Result

An image of a correctly colored apple appears around the dot. This image will appear in a flash at first, but be patient—the image soon returns so that you can see it more clearly. Depending on how steady your stare was, this image will have either sharp or blurred edges.

Explanation

Light is perceived in the part of the eye called the retina. The retina is covered with light-sensitive cells called rods and cones, each set of which has a specific function. The rods are useful for night vision because they are less sensitive to color and more sensitive to the subtle contrasts of light you see in the dark. (That's why your eyes "hurt" when you come from a dark place into bright light.) The cones are less sensitive to contrast in light and more sensitive to color.

Staring at a particular color, say green, for too long fatigues the green-sensitive cones in your retina because you force them to continually produce the electrochemical signal "green" to the brain. When you finally look away, the cones "relax" by producing a signal for red, the complementary color of green. If you stare at yellow too long, the cones relax by producing blue. The phenomenon of color afterimage means that whichever color exhausts the cones of your eye will cause them to produce the complementary rather than the exhausting color.

Did You Know?

The "green flash"—real or an illusion? Many people claim to see a green flash in the seconds immediately following a sunset. The descriptions vary from a localized flash at the point on the horizon where the sun disappears to a change of hue in the entire sky. Knowing what you now know about the color afterimage effect, can you think of a scientific explanation for this phenomenon?

Phenakistoscope Animation

You Will Need

- 12-inch (30-cm) -square corrugated cardboard
- ¼ × 6-inch (0.62 × 20-cm) wooden dowel
- 2 wooden ball ornaments with predrilled holes that fit dowel's ends
- 2 wire coat hangers
- 12-inch (30-cm) -square wood or Styrofoam for platform
- 12-inch (30-cm) -square free-standing mirror
- Craft knife
- Ruler
- Pencil
- String
- Felt-tip marking pen
- White paper
- Black paint
- Paintbrush
- Nail
- Wire cutters
- Pliers
- Drafting compass

Phenakistoscope

Wheel Construction

Procedure

1. Tie one end of the string to the pencil. Place the cardboard on a flat, firm surface. With one finger, hold the free end of the string down near the center of the cardboard. Use your other hand to hold the pencil and stretch the string taut. Twist the pencil until the string is about 5 inches (12.5 cm) long. Then sweep the pencil around to draw a perfect 10-inch (25-cm) -diameter circle.

2. Use the felt-tip marking pen and ruler to draw 12 equally spaced lines on the edge of the circle. Make each line 1 inch (2.5 cm) long.

3. Use the craft knife and ruler to carefully cut slots over each line. Each slot should be just wide enough to peek through. Use the nail to carefully punch a hole in the circle where your finger depressed the cardboard.

4. Paint the circle black and allow the paint to dry.

The art of animation is based on the brain's inability to differentiate sequentially related visual elements when the elements are flashed or pulsed above a certain speed. All animation media, from the simple flipbook to 70-mm film, take advantage of this persistence of vision. The phenakistoscope, or "deceiver device," was a popular animation novelty about 100 years ago.

5. Place the dowel through the hole in the center of the cardboard, and push a wooden ball ornament over each end of the dowel.

6. Unbend 2 coat hangers so that you have two 9-inch (22.5-cm) lengths of wire. Bend the tops of the wires into hooks (see illustration on page 90). Push 1 inch (2.5 cm) of the straight end of each wire into the Styrofoam block or drill a hole in the wood and insert the wires.

7. Suspend the dowel on the wire hooks, making sure that the cardboard circle can rotate freely.

8. Place a mirror at one end of the mechanism.

Animation Discs

Procedure

1. With the ruler, measure the distance between the circle's center and the inner edge of a slot (about 4 inches or 10 cm).

2. Use the compass and marker to draw a circle with a 4-inch (10-cm) diameter on the white paper. Draw 3 smaller concentric circles inside the 5-inch (12.5-cm) circle. In light pencil, draw a series of X's inside the circles (see diagram below). Notice how the X's are arranged in circles also.

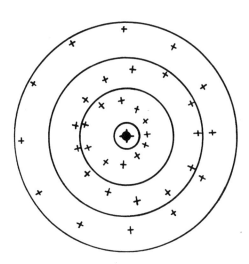

Phenakistoscope Disc

3. Punch a hole in the center of the circle where the compass needle made a mark; then cut out the circle. Since the circle will be the drawing pad for your animation, make quite a few photocopies of the circle and cut out each one.

4. Again, note the X's arranged in circles. Over each X in a circle, make a small drawing. The drawing can be larger than the X, of course, but it shouldn't stray into the area of a neighboring X. Also, each drawing in a circle should relate to the previous drawing, as if you were drawing pages in a flipbook.

Operating the Phenakistoscope

Procedure

1. Remove an ornament from one end of the dowel, and push a completed paper disc along the dowel until it sits against the record. You may have to attach a little tape to the disc to keep it from folding over. Replace the wooden-ball ornament.

2. Turn the phenakistoscope so that the drawing faces the mirror. Spin the cardboard circle and look through the slots at your drawing reflected in the mirror.

Result

The drawings in the series of circles combine to create 3 rows of continuous animation.

Explanation

All animation is the simulation of movement by flashing separate images at the eye at speeds greater than it can process. At a speed exceeding $\frac{1}{16}$ of a second, the eye and brain are unable to distinguish individual images and blend them together into one contiguous image of motion.

Television-Screen Phosphorescence

You Will Need

- Television
- Flashlight
- Black construction paper
- White paper
- Dark room

A television screen produces extremely complex images in fractions of a second. However, the construction of the screen is relatively simple and relies on a phenomenon familiar to you if you've ever looked at your wristwatch or alarm clock in the dark.

Procedure

1. Make the room with the television very dark. Stand in the room long enough for your eyes to get accustomed to the dark.

2. Holding the flashlight, stand about 5 feet (1.5 m) from the front of the television.

3. Close your eyes tightly, switch on the flashlight, and wave it slowly back and forth in the direction of the television screen. Then turn off the flashlight and open your eyes. What do you see?

4. Close your eyes again, then switch the television on and off quickly. Open your eyes and look at the television screen.

5. With the light back on, cut a small square from the center of the black construction paper and tape a square of white paper over the square. The white paper square should be slightly larger than the square you cut.

6. Tape the construction paper to the center of the television screen; then turn off the room lights and allow your eyes to adjust to the dark.

7. Close your eyes and turn on the television. This time leave it on for about 2 minutes. Then turn it off and look at the screen.

Result

Waving the flashlight back and forth created a green glowing stripe across the screen that traced the flashlight's path. Switching the television on and off made the entire screen glow, brightly enough to see your hand. Taping the construction paper to the screen resulted in something curious: The white paper glowed a whitish green almost as if it were a television screen itself.

Explanation

The image on a television screen is produced by a stream of changing electrons from an electron gun that fan out and cover the inside of the screen. The interior surface of the screen is coated with a microscopically thin layer of phosphorus compound that absorbs the electron energy and turns it into light. The phosphorus also retains the light after the light source is removed. Scientists call this kind of chemical light retention phosphorescence, and you saw it clearly when you waved the flashlight and switched the television on and off. The black construction paper absorbed electrons passing through the television screen while the white paper reflected them back. This means that the white paper stimulated the phosphorus from both directions, making the screen glow more brightly in the area covered by white paper.

Additive & Subtractive Colors

<table>
<tr><td>

You Will Need

- Computer monitor
- Color picture from a magazine
- Magnifying glass
- Red, blue, green, and yellow tempera paint
- Paintbrushes
- Colored pencils
- White paper

</td></tr>
</table>

You might think that mixing colors is easily done with a few crayons or paints. But this project will show you that the science of making color follows some important rules, depending on the medium.

Procedure

1. Find an image on your computer screen with plenty of purple and orange.

2. Hold a magnifying glass up to something purple on the screen until the purple breaks up into little squares, or pixels. (Hint: you'll see colors other than purple.)

3. Use colored pencils to make a few dots on the white paper, corresponding to the colored pixels you see on the screen. Label the group of dots "purple."

4. Repeat steps #2 and 3 for something orange.

5. Look at your first group of dots labeled "purple." Mix tempera paints in the same color combination as the dots. Do the colors combine to make purple? Repeat this procedure for orange.

6. Choose a picture from a magazine with purples and oranges. Hold a magnifying glass to each color, and make a dot sketch as before. Then combine the tempera paints using the dot sketches as a guide. Do you get the colors you expect?

7. Hold the magnifying glass up to something on the computer screen that looks pure white. Do the same for the magazine picture. Record your observations.

Result

On the computer screen, the purple is made from the combination of blue, green, and red dots. The orange is made by combining red and green dots. (The color combinations will vary slightly depending on the exact shade of color you choose and how your monitor processes the color information.) But when you mix these colors with the tempera paint, you wind up with two shades of brown. The magazine picture gets its color by combining cyan (turquoise), magenta (purple-red), yellow, and black. This is called four-color printing.

When you examine the magazine purples and oranges, you see that the purple is created by combining magenta and cyan dots and the orange is made from magenta and yellow dots. Mixing these colors in tempera produces similar shades of purple and orange.

When you magnified the white on the computer screen and compared it with the magazine white, you saw that the screen white is made from combining red, green, and blue pixels! The magazine white has little, if any, color.

Explanation

Computer screens and magazine pictures display color in two different ways. A computer screen shows color in the form of emanated light, while a magazine picture shows color in absorbed and reflected light. Using light to make different colors is called additive color mixing; using absorption and reflection to make colors is called subtractive color mixing. With an additive color like yellow, the wavelengths of green and red combine (add) and interfere to create yellow. But a subtractive yellow absorbs (subtracts) all other colors of the spectrum and reflects back only yellow to our eyes.

Reproducing the color combinations you saw on the screen with paint yielded a poor result because paint is a subtractive color medium. You had more success using the paint to create the colors you saw in the magazine.

Strobe Effect of a Computer Monitor

You Will Need

- Computer monitor or television screen
- Something crunchy to chew on
- Dimmed room

The phosphorescing screen of a computer or television was designed to fool your eye into seeing one continuous image. This is based on the fact that most people sit when watching screen images. But with a little movement, you can easily see around this illusion. Although you can do this experiment with either a computer monitor or a television screen, the effect will be heightened with a steady image rather than a moving one.

Procedure

1. Turn on your computer monitor and dim the lights. Stand about 12 feet (3.6 m) from the screen.

2. Stand still and look at the screen for a few moments. Then pop something crunchy in your mouth and, while chewing, stare at the screen, focusing on one spot. Finish chewing and swallowing before proceeding to the next step.

3. Without bounding up and down too much, jog in place while staring at the screen.

4. Wiggle your head from side to side while staring at the screen.

Result

Each of your movements causes the screen image to break into bands of light and dark, or even to flicker.

Explanation

The chewing, jogging, and wiggling all caused your head to vibrate rapidly. This means that the image of the screen on your retina vibrated also. This isn't a problem for ordinary images, but a computer image is a kind of strobe light that flickers on and off about 60 times each second. Your brain becomes a little confused with both sets of data—the vibrating retina image and a flickering screen image—and can't process the visual information as effectively as it normally would.

Pencil Test for Computer-Screen Refresh Rate

You Will Need

- Computer monitor or television screen
- Pencil

By experimenting with different types of motion in front of a computer screen, you can begin to understand how the screen creates images. The result will vary depending on the kind and size of your monitor, so you may have to try this several times, even darkening the room to heighten the effect if necessary.

Procedure

1. Turn on your computer monitor. Allow the screen to display a simple image with a uniform color.

2. Sit close to the monitor and hold a pencil up to the screen, practically touching it. Hold the pencil so that it points up and crosses the middle of the screen.

3. Focus your eyes on some detail of the screen behind the pencil; then move the pencil back and forth across the screen, following the pencil's tip without directly watching it. Slowly increase the back-and-forth movement until you are swinging the pencil as fast as you can; then stop.

4. Hold the pencil so that it points to one side of the screen. Repeat step #3, this time moving the pencil up and down instead of from side to side. Record your observations.

Result

Both motions broke the movement of the pencil into little "snapshots" of the pencil's movement across the screen. Although moving the pencil up and down across the screen had no noticeable effect on the pencil's shape, moving it back and forth gave the illusion that the tip of the pencil was bending in the direction opposite its movement. This illusion was heightened the faster you moved the pencil.

Explanation

When you look at a computer or television screen, you aren't seeing a steady image, but a flickering strobe effect that redraws or refreshes itself from top to bottom. This refresh rate is measured in cycles called megahertz (MHz) and happens so quickly that the human eye perceives one continuous image. The average computer screen refreshes at a rate of 60 MHz, which means that the light flickers about 60 times each second. Since the image is redrawn from top to bottom, the back-and-forth motion of the pencil was distorted because the top and bottom of the pencil were stopped at different times.

Wheatstone 3-D Viewer

You Will Need

- 8 × 10-inch (20 × 25-cm) stereo-scopic photo pair (see "Free-Viewing Stereoscopic Pairs")
- Two 8 × 10-inch (20 × 25-cm) acrylic mirrors
- Two 8 × 10-inch (20 × 25-cm) cardboard squares
- 4 paper clips
- Masking tape
- Craft knife
- Table and chair

This project requires that you enlarge a pair of homemade stereoscopic photographs. You can also make stereoscopic drawings for your viewer, but a carefully composed photograph will provide enhanced perspective for a much more dramatic effect. You can use monochromes as well as color prints, but for the best result in black and white, select a photo that has pronounced contrast and fewer gray tones.

Three-dimensional, or stereoscopic, photographs were once enjoyed by millions. Although the principles of human stereoscopic vision were discussed in the early 1800s, no method existed to prove the theories until Sir Charles Wheatstone invented his Wheatstone Viewer

and demonstrated it to the British Royal Society in 1838. The device was simple: two large mirrors hinged together allowed the viewer to place his face at the joint and experience the stereography of merged images. Reflected in each mirror was one of a pair of large stereographic photographs that, when combined by the eye and brain, produced a single three-dimensional scene.

Procedure

1. Place the mirrors together on the table, reflecting side down. Use a piece of masking tape to attach the long edges of the mirrors together. Trim the excess tape with the craft knife.

2. Tape a piece of cardboard to each outside edge of the joined mirrors. Trim the excess tape.

3. Stand the taped mirrors and cardboards on their edges with the reflecting sides of the mirrors facing you. You should have an accordion-shaped viewer with the joined

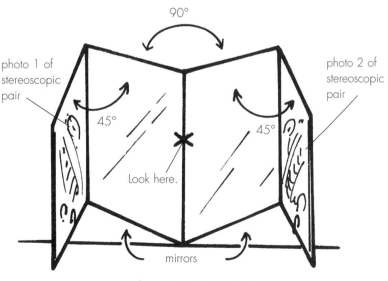

Wheatstone Viewer Setup

mirrors at the center (the center joint). Make sure the hinges are loose enough so that you can adjust the shape of your viewer.

4. With paper clips, attach a photograph to each of the outside cardboard pieces. Each photograph should completely cover the cardboard.

5. Pull the viewer close to the end of the table so that you can position your face at the center joint of the mirrors. Fold the mirrors back to a 90-degree angle.

6. Fold each photograph to a 45-degree angle from its mirror. The photographs should wind up parallel and with their edges facing you.

7. To see the photographs merge into one 3-D view, place your face directly in front of the center joint. You may have to adjust the angle of mirrors and photographs until you see a single, seamless reflection in the mirrors. Don't try to focus, but allow your eyes to relax until the images merge into one three-dimensional view.

Result

For a while, one reflected image will appear to float over the other, but eventually the images will come together—with a startling result. Remember, a stereoscopic pair consists of two slightly different views of the same object. This subtle shift in perspective between the two photos simulates the degree of displacement between the views from each of your eyes. When the viewer's mirrors superimpose the photographs and force you to see them as one, the brain is fooled.

Tabletop Stereoscope

You Will Need

- 2 small pocket mirrors, same size
- 2 pieces of thick plywood, cut slightly smaller than mirrors *(mounts)*
- 2 pieces of plywood, cut slightly smaller than mirrors *(bases)*
- Two 1 × 3 × 5-inch (2.5 × 7.5 × 12.5-cm) wooden blocks
- Two 5 × 9-inch (12.5 × 22.5-cm) pieces Masonite or thin plywood
- 4 metal L-shape brackets and screws to fit
- 4 wood screws
- 4 rubber bands
- Pair of stereoscopic drawings or photographs (see "Free-Viewing Stereoscopic Pairs")

From the mid-1800s to the 1930s, stereoscopic photographs were created and enjoyed by millions. Although the principles of human stereoscopic vision were discussed in the early 1800s, no method existed to prove the theories until Sir Charles Wheatstone invented a device of angled mirrors. Hinged together and adjustable, the large mirrors were used with a pair of carefully displaced photographs, that, when observed through the Wheatstone Viewer, produced a perfectly rendered scene in three dimensions (3-D). This project replicates Wheatstone's device as a table model.

Procedure

1. Center and glue two of the plywood mounts to the backs of the mirrors so that no more than ¼ inch (0.62 cm) of mirror protrudes along each edge.

2. Measure the longer sides of each plywood piece, and make a pencil mark along the edge at the midpoint.

3. Screw the long end of each L-shaped bracket to the pencil marks with the shorter end facing in. Screw the shorter ends into the plywood bases. Tighten the screws at the bases, but make sure that the mounted mirrors can swivel.

4. To make the mounting boards for the stereoscopic pictures, screw the 5-inch (12.5-cm) sides of the Masonite strips to the 5-inch (12.5-cm) sides of the wooden blocks.

Tabletop Stereoscope

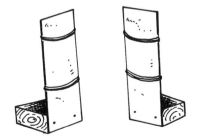

Plywood Mounting Boards

5. Stand the boards upright on their blocks, and loop two rubber bands around each.

6. Place the mounting boards at opposite sides of the finished viewer. Each board should face a mirror from a distance of about 8 inches (20 cm).

7. To operate the viewer, place a stereoscopic drawing or photograph sideways on each mounting board with the top of the picture pointing away from you. Secure the picture with rubber bands.

8. Stand directly over the viewer and look down into the mirrors. Adjust the mirrors so that you see two pictures, one appearing to float on top of the other. Move the pictures if necessary so that they completely fill the mirrors.

9. Relax your eyes and allow the two pictures to flow together.

Result

The two pictures merge into one three-dimensional scene. This scene vanishes the moment you tilt one of the mirrors or move one of the mounted pictures.

Explanation

The mirrors send two slightly different views of the same scene to your brain. The degree of displacement between the two pictures simulates the degree of displacement between the view from each eye. The brain interprets this binocular vision in three dimensions (3-D).

Free-Viewing Stereoscopic Pairs

You Will Need

- 35-mm camera (disposable camera OK)
- Tracing paper
- Pencil
- Pen
- Ruler

A stereoscopic pair consists of two photographs or drawings of exactly the same thing, except that the view in one photo is slightly displaced from the view in the other photo. Each photograph simulates the separate view from each eye that the brain combines into one three-dimensional scene. Although the principles of stereoscopic vision were understood, and stereoscopic pairs were created in the early 1800s, no device existed to view them easily until Sir Charles Wheatstone invented his Wheatstone Viewer in 1838. Before the viewer, those wishing to enjoy stereo pairs had to learn to free-view them. In this project, you'll create stereoscopic pairs of photographs and drawings and free-view them.

You can also view your pairs on a stereoscopic viewer. (See "Wheatstone 3-D Viewer" and "Tabletop Stereoscope" projects.)

Stereoscopic Drawings

Procedure

1. Look at drawings A and B. Notice the four planes of perspective in each drawing—fence, lamb, hill, barn, and clouds—and how the fence, lamb, hill, barn, and clouds have been moved to the right in drawing B.

2. You could place any object in each of the four planes, but the farther back an object is in drawing A, the more it must be moved to the right in drawing B.

3. To start a new stereoscopic pair, place a piece of tracing paper over drawing A and draw five new objects with the first object closest to you and the fifth object farthest away. Use this as your new drawing A.

4. Place a piece of tracing paper over the new drawing A. Trace the object closest to you in exactly the same position. Then move the tracing paper ⅛ inch (0.31 cm) to the left and trace the next object. Move the paper ⅛ inch (0.31 cm) to the left again and trace the next object, and so on, until you've traced all the objects of drawing A onto drawing B.

A   B

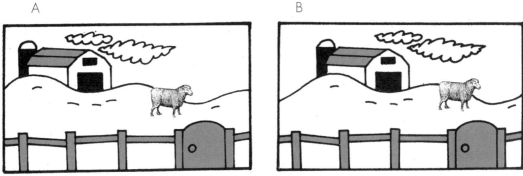

Stereoscopic Drawings

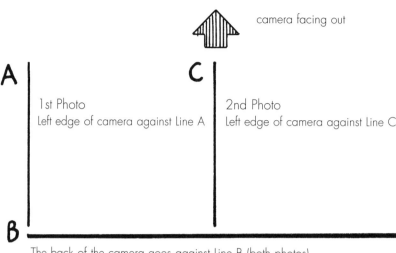

camera facing out

A

1st Photo
Left edge of camera against Line A

C

2nd Photo
Left edge of camera against Line C

B

The back of the camera goes against Line B (both photos).
Place camera on its side for vertical photographs.

Camera Guide

5. Cut the pictures out and tape them with their sides touching to a piece of cardboard.

Stereoscopic Photographs

Procedure

1. Use the camera guide to position your camera for each photograph of the stereoscopic pair. Photocopy the guide from the book; then place the guide on a level surface with the arrow pointing toward you. You can use the guide to take either horizontal or vertical photographs. For vertical photos, stand the camera on its side.

2. Place the back of your camera against line B and the left side of your camera against line A.

3. Instruct your subject to stand about 5 feet (1.5 m) in front of you, or focus on something 5 feet (1.5 m) away. Take the first photo.

4. With the back of the camera still against line B, move the camera so that its left side now touches line C. Make sure your subject doesn't move, and take the second photo.

5. Tape the developed photos with their sides touching on a piece of cardboard.

Free-Viewing

Procedure

1. Focus on some object about 20 feet (6 m) away. While looking at that object, slowly move the cardboard containing the drawings or photographs in front of you to a distance of about 1 foot (30 cm).

2. Allow your eyes to see double images, and don't force your eyes to bring the images together. Instead, relax your eyes and concentrate on the fuzzy area where the two images seem to overlap. If your eyes suddenly focus and you see two separate pictures, repeat step #1.

Result
With a little practice, the fuzzy area of overlapping pictures will suddenly come together into a single stereo view.

Explanation
When relaxed, your eyes will stop trying to see each picture individually and fuse them together to create a single stereo view. This occurs because you view the pair obliquely, with your focus directed to some virtual object beyond the cardboard.

Light & Sound

Explore Virtual Harmony with a Harmonograph

You Will Need

- ¾ × ¾ × 38-inch square wooden dowel
- ¾ × ¾ × 44-inch square wooden dowel
- ¾ × ¾ × 10-inch square wooden dowel (platform braces)
- ⅞ × ⅞ × 9-inch square wooden dowel, cut in half
- 14 × 22-inch (35 × 55-cm) clear acrylic sheet
- Two 1 × 3 × 21-inch boards
- Two 1 × 3 × 13-inch boards
- Four 2 × 2 × 36-inch-square wooden posts
- Wooden yardstick, meterstick, or paint stirrer (disposable)
- 10 × 10-inch (25 × 25-cm) -square thin plywood or Masonite (platform)
- Two 1 × 3-inch (2.5 × 7.5-cm) strips thin copper

- Eight 1½-inch flat-head wood-screws
- Eight ¾-inch flat-head wood-screws
- 10 machine screws and washers
- 8 nails
- Wing-nut screw with 3 metal washers
- 2 adjustable circle braces with screws
- Fine-point felt-tip marking pen
- Masking tape
- Two 4-fluid-ounce (120-ml) paper cups
- Plaster of paris
- Petroleum jelly
- Drill
- Miter saw
- Skill saw
- Craft knife
- Large binder clip
- Pencil
- Vellum paper

This project will allow you to construct a device that enjoyed great popularity during the turn of the century—the harmonograph. Victorian science enthusiasts would marvel at the combined motion of its dual pendulums tracing intricate patterns on paper. Far from just a novelty item, however, the harmono-graph demonstrated important principles of *periodic harmonic motion.* Simplified, this law states that a pendulum pulled 45° from its rest-ing position and released will swing 45° in the opposite direction from its resting position. The motion repeats itself and is periodic until the pendulum loses momentum and stops.

The number of swings per unit of time is the pendulum's frequency. This means that a shorter pendulum swinging rapidly has a higher frequency than a long, slow-swinging pendulum. By comparing the frequencies of two swinging pendulums you'll discover the real fascination of the harmonograph. Since frequency describes vibration, a swinging pendulum virtually "vibrates"—much like a ringing tone—although at a much, much slower speed. In fact, a dual-pendulum harmonograph is actually showing us the combination of two greatly slowed down musical tones, or harmonies.

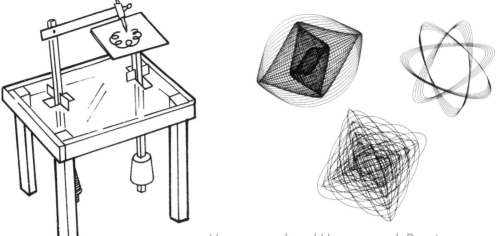

Harmonograph and Harmonograph Drawings

Harmonic Secrets

When two tones are sounded together, the effect is either consonant (pleasant) or dissonant (unpleasant). Over 2,000 years ago, the Greek philosopher Pythagoras discovered that the pleasing experience of musical harmony results when the ratio between the frequencies of two plucked strings is small, such as 1:1, 2:1, or 3:2. When the ratio is high, dissonance results.

The musical scale used in the West is based on Pythagoras' discovery. The scale consists of a series of octaves in each of which the highest tone (octave) has a frequency double that of the lowest tone (unison). Although each octave contains twelve tones, it's the seven tones of the diatonic scale that interest us here. The chart shows each of these seven tones and their ratio to the unison tone.

The harmonograph translates the harmonic relationships shown in the chart into visual form. It does this with two pendulums, one with the weight kept at its lowest point, while the weight on the other is moved to wherever it will produce the required ratio. In this way, two vibrations are combined into a single drawing, just as two musical tones sounded together produce harmony.

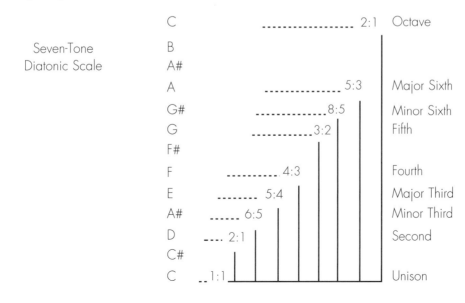

Seven-Tone Diatonic Scale

C	2:1	Octave
B		
A#		
A	5:3	Major Sixth
G#	8:5	Minor Sixth
G	3:2	Fifth
F#		
F	4:3	Fourth
E	5:4	Major Third
A#	6:5	Minor Third
D	2:1	Second
C#		
C	1:1	Unison

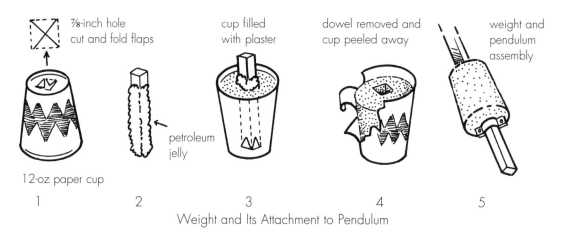

⅞-inch hole
cut and fold flaps

cup filled
with plaster

dowel removed and
cup peeled away

weight and
pendulum
assembly

petroleum
jelly

12-oz paper cup

1   2   3   4   5

Weight and Its Attachment to Pendulum

The Stylus & Platform Pendulums

Procedure

1. Cut the 9-inch wooden dowel into two equal halves. Turn one of the paper cups over, and trace the end of the dowel onto the bottom of the paper cup so that you have a centered ⅞-inch (2.2-cm) square. Cut diagonally across the square and fold the flaps down, following the diagram. Repeat this procedure for the second cup.

2. Place a sheet of waxed paper on the tabletop. Apply a coating of petroleum jelly to each of the 4½-inch wooden dowels, almost to the top.

3. Stand the cups upright and place a 4½-inch wooden dowel into each cup, greased end down. The ends of the dowels should fit into the flaps of the holes.

4. Add ½ cup (120 ml) of sand to 8 ounces (225 g) of plaster. Stir the plaster until it looks like putty, then spoon the plaster into the paper cups while holding the dowels upright. Allow the plaster to set around the dowels.

5. After the plaster dries, carefully peel the cups away from the set molds, and then gently remove the dowels. You should have two plaster weights with ⅞-inch (2.2-cm) square openings at the center of each.

6. Measure and mark 32 inches (80 cm) from the bottoms of the 44-inch and 38-inch wooden dowels. These are the fulcrum points for the pendulums. Mark "0" at the fulcrum points and "32 inches" (80 cm) at the pendulums' bottoms.

fulcrum

weight

Intervals on Pendulum

Interval		Length from Fulcrum
2:1	Octave	20.1 cm
3:3	Major Sixth	23.9 cm
3:5	Minor Sixth	31.6 cm
3:2	Fifth	35.9 cm
4:3	Fourth	45.0 cm
5:4	Major Third	52.5 cm
6:5	Minor Third	55.7 cm
9:8	Second	64.0 cm
1:1	Unison	80 cm

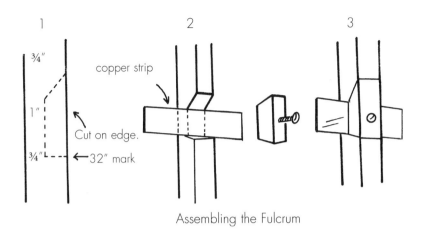

Assembling the Fulcrum

7. Draw bold lines along each pendulum following the measurements in the diagram.

8. Start with the 38-inch (95-cm) pendulum. Measuring up from the 32-inch (80-cm) mark, cut a wedge-shaped piece from the dowel using the skill saw (see dimensions below). Insert the copper strip lengthwise, centering it on the dowel. Replace the wedge, wrap a piece of masking tape around the top to secure it, then carefully drill through the wedge, strip, and dowel so that you can insert a screw and attach all the pieces together. Repeat this procedure for the 44-inch (110-cm) pendulum.

9. Take the 44-inch (110-cm) pendulum and measure 1½ inch (3.75 cm) from the top

(the top is the shorter distance from the ful- crum). Drill a hole in the cen- ter of the dowel large enough to allow a wing- nut screw to pass through.

10. Cut the disposable yardstick down to 12 inches (30 cm). Measure 1 inch (2.5 cm) from the end, and drill a hole with the same dimensions as the hole in the dowel.

11. Attach the yardstick to the dowel with the wing-nut screw and washers, following the diagram. Make sure the yardstick pivots freely against the pendulum.

12. Draw diagonal lines connecting the corners of the 10 × 10-inch (25 × 25-cm) plat- form. The crossing lines indicate the center of the platform. Attach the end of the 38-inch wooden dowel to this center point with a flat-head screw.

13. Place a plaster weight at the bottom of each pendulum, and attach an adjustable circle brace to keep the weights from slipping.

Construction of the Table

Procedure

1. Nail the 1 × 3-inch boards together in a rectangle, and attach a square post to each corner with two 1½-inch screws (see the dia- gram). Make sure the table sits level, adding a furniture coaster to the bottom of each post if necessary.

2. Use the drill and skill saw to cut two 1 × 3-inch (2.5 × 7.5-cm) rectangular holes into the 14 × 22-inch (35 × 55-cm) clear acrylic sheet. Then place the sheet over the table, and drill 10 small holes along its perimeter. Attach the sheet to the table with machine screws and washers.

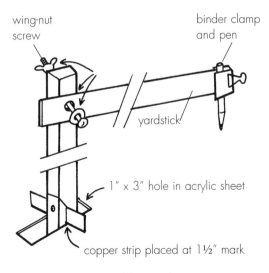

Pendulum Stylus

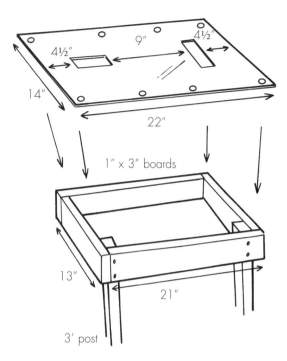

Table Assembly

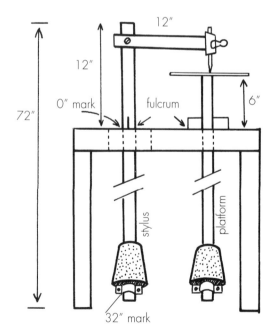

Harmonograph Setup

Assembly & Operation

Procedure

1. Remove the weights from the bottoms of the pendulums. Slip the stylus pendulum into the horizontal hole in the acrylic sheet and position the copper-strip fulcrum so that it sits at the exact center of the hole.

2. Slip the platform pendulum into the vertical hole in the acrylic sheet and center the copper-strip fulcrum. You should have two balanced pendulums, the stylus pendulum swinging horizontally and the platform pendulum swinging vertically.

3. Wrap masking tape around the center of the pen, and attach the pen to the end of the yardstick with the large binder clip.

4. To insure a smooth surface, tape the corners of the 10×10-inch (25×25-cm) cardboard to the wooden platform of the platform pendulum. Then tape a square piece of smooth vellum paper to the cardboard.

5. Reattach the weights to the bottoms of the pendulums, and check to make sure that the point of the pen sits in the center of the paper. You may have to adjust the fulcrum positions of the pendulums to get everything to line up correctly.

6. To operate the harmonograph, pull both pendulums back to their highest points. Release one pendulum, then release the other when the first is at its mid-point. Allow the motions of the pendulums to combine, recorded in a drawing made by the action of the pen on the paper.

7. Leave the weight in position on the stylus pendulum, but move the weight up to the next mark on the platform pendulum. Repeat step #6.

8. Continue to move the platform weight up along the pendulum. Collect the drawings and compare them.

Result

Each combination of tones or intervals creates a distinct pattern. The more complex patterns emerge when combining tones with greater ratios.

A Foam-Board Phonograph

You Will Need

- 10-inch (25-cm) phonograph record (*don't use one you're afraid to damage*)
- 12 × 24-inch (30 × 60-cm) foam board
- Metal hatpin or steel phonograph needle
- 2 pencils
- Yardstick or meterstick
- Craft knife
- Saw
- Transparent tape
- 2 pencils
- Large nail
- Wire clippers

Foam-Board Phonograph

Sound waves travel more efficiently through many solids than they do through air. But a sound wave must eventually travel through air to reach our ears. This means that the vibrations in a solid medium must be translated into compression waves in air so that the sound can reach our eardrums. In this project, this process is explored through the construction of a foam-board phonograph.

Procedure

1. Use the pencil and yardstick to divide the foam board into three 8 × 12-inch (20 × 30-cm) sections. With the craft knife, make small notches in the foam board where the line meets the edges.

2. Turn the foam board over and lay the edge of the yardstick from notch to notch. With the craft knife, carefully score (cut through the paper layer only) the foam board between the two notches.

3. Turn the foam board over and carefully bend it toward you along the scores until you have a folding-tent shape.

4. With the saw, cut off the eraser end of the pencil, just before the metal band.

5. Use the large nail to make a hole in the foam board in the position indicated. Widen the hole with the nail until you can push in the piece of pencil so that it fits snugly with the eraser side up. This is the spindle.

6. Measure 2 inches (5 cm) from the right along the bottom edge of the third piece of foam board and mark the place with the pencil.

7. Clip the hatpin down to 1 inch (2.5 cm) or use a 1-inch steel phonograph needle.

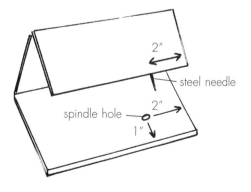

Preparing Foam Board

Wrap a narrow strip of transparent tape around the blunt end of the hatpin and carefully insert this end directly into the edge of the foam board.

8. Brush some rubber cement over a portion of the record's label. The cement creates a good gripping place for turning the record, and can easily be scraped off later.

9. To operate, place the record on the spindle and adjust the cardboard so that the needle sits at the edge of the record. Hold the foam board with one hand, and spin the record clockwise with the other hand by pressing the eraser end of the pencil against the glued part of the label.

Result

As you spin the record, you can hear music coming from the triangular hollow made by the folded foam board.

Explanation

This simple device produces sound by means of a record, needle reproducer, resonator, and conducting medium.

Record & Needle: As the needle runs over the grooves in the record's surface, it vibrates at various frequencies determined by the size and shape of the grooves. This technique of analog sound reproduction translates information from one physical quantity (record grooves) into another physical quantity (needle vibrations).

Reproducer & Resonator: The vibrations in the needle have such a low amplitude (volume) that you can't hear them very well. Some method is needed to conduct the vibrations away from the needle and into something larger that will resonate more powerfully. The piece of foam board that contains the needle serves this purpose. By acting as a reproducer, the foam board reproduces the vibrations of the needle with greater amplitude.

But to truly be heard, the vibrations need a resonator or some kind of container that will allow the vibrations to move from the foam board into the conducting medium of air. The chamber of the resonator should have a design that supports the vibrations and allows their amplitude to increase even further. The resonating chamber of your phonograph is the triangular space created by the folded foam board and foam-board base. From here, the sound travels out in compression waves that reach your ears.

Did You Know?

Early acoustic phonographs reproduced sound without the use of electricity. These elegant machines operated on the simple transference of vibrations you examined above. Look at a picture of an old wind-up phonograph. Although the machine appears to have many parts, can you identify the needle, reproducer, and resonator?

Shifting Phase Relationships in Tuning Forks

You Will Need

- 2 tuning forks, same size
- 2 tin cans, same size
- Plywood board
- Four 1 × 1 × 6-inch wood strips
- Scrap wood block, same diameter as tin cans
- White glue
- Transparent tape
- Can opener
- Ruler
- Drill

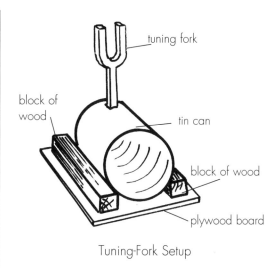

Tuning-Fork Setup

Sound waves, like any other type of wave, can either complement or interfere with one another. With light waves, this interference can result in the shifting array of colors on the surface of a soap bubble. With sound, the interference results in the phase phenomenon demonstrated by this project.

Forks & Resonators

Procedure

1. Use the can opener to remove the bottoms of the tin cans.

2. Measure the diameter of the cans with the ruler, and then glue the wood strips on the board so that each pair of strips cradles a tin can and keeps it from moving. Allow the glue to dry.

3. Insert the block of wood into one of the cans. The wood should be snug enough to press against the sides.

4. Turn the can on its side, and with the block of wood supporting the can, drill a hole in the side of the can. The hole should be large enough to receive the end of the tuning fork, but small enough to keep the fork from slipping down. Repeat this procedure for the other can.

5. Place the cans in their cradles with the holes facing up.

Comparing Phases

Procedure

1. Wrap a piece of transparent tape around one of the prongs of one tuning fork.

2. Pick up both forks, and strike both against the edge of the wood at the same time.

3. Quickly place each fork in its hole in the tin can. Listen and describe what you hear.

Result

A distinct pulsing sound results from the combined rings of the forks. The pulse is loud, then faint, then loud, then faint again and continues until the forks lose their vibration.

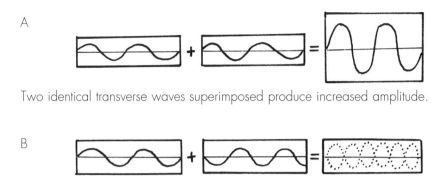

A

Two identical transverse waves superimposed produce increased amplitude.

B

Two out-of-phase transverse waves superimposed cancel each other out.

Explanation

The forks produce two different frequencies of sound that combine and produce the pulse effect. This is because the vibrations of the forks will be momentarily in step, then out of step, then in again, and so on. When the combined waves reach your ears in step, they are in phase and the sound is loudest.

Since a sound of a particular frequency, or pitch, produces a distinct wavelength, a second sound with its own distinct wavelength can interfere with the first sound's wavelength. The diagram below shows that when the crest of one wave matches and overlaps the crest of another wave, a louder sound results. But when the crest of one wave overlaps the trough of another, the sound you hear is softer.

Did You Know?

Using Sound to Make Silence: The concept of interference has led to some interesting ideas for new technologies. Since it's possible for waves to overlap so that a smaller composite sound results, it's theoretically possible to create waves that completely neutralize each other so that their combined effect is no sound at all! The idea of using destructive interference to create silence is fascinating and has already been attempted with encouraging results. Scientists, studying the sound of a noisy machine shop, used a computer to create a "negative image" of that sound. When this computer-generated sound was beamed at the ambient noise of the shop, a nearly total silence was produced.

Birefringence in a Sheet of Cellophane

You Will Need

- 2 small glass sheets from photo frames
- 2 polarized filters *(science supply store)*
- Cellophane
- White light or sunlight
- Masking tape
- Transparent tape

This project demonstrates the unusual optical qualities of certain cellophane plastics. These plastics, in turn, imitate the light-refracting behavior of a variety of crystals found in nature.

Some materials have the ability to alter light waves in usual ways. Physicists call these materials *birefringent*, which means that when light enters them, it refracts (bends) twice and in two different directions. When you look through a strongly birefringent material like calcite, you see a double image. In fact, when a calcite crystal is held over a piece of newsprint, the print is visible not only through the crystal as you would expect, but also just below the upper surface, as if projected there.

Birefringence is a property of noncubic or anisotropic crystals. Unlike cubic or isotropic crystals, birefringent crystals (including liquid crystals) have a molecular structure that allows them to split light, not only in two directions and along two planes, but also into fast- and slow-moving waves called ordinary and extraordinary. As these waves move through the birefringent material, they have the potential to interfere with one another and to produce an array of shifting colors—viewable only through a pair of polarized filters.

Many synthetic materials such as glass and plastic have birefringent properties because their molecular structure mimics that of an anisotropic crystal. To view the birefringent effect, light is made to shine through the material and then through the first polarized filter, or polarizer. The light from the polarizer is then viewed through the second filter, called the analyzer.

Procedure

1. Wrinkle up a piece of cellophane and place it between two pieces of glass.

2. Put masking tape around the edges of the glass pieces to seal them together.

3. Attach the first polarized filter (polarizer) to the glass with a little transparent tape.

4. Prop the glass between two stacks of books with the polarized filter side facing you.

5. Place the lamp behind the glass, about 3 feet (90 cm) away.

6. Look at the glass through the second polarized filter (analyzer). Slowly rotate the filter and record your observations.

Result

The portion of cellophane visible through the polarizer is covered in changing colors. This is true even for the slivers of transparent tape that overlap the polarizer. As you rotate the analyzer, the colors appear to mutate and shift positions.

Explanation

Cellophane is composed of chain molecules that behave optically like the molecules of anisotropic crystals. In other words, cellophane is birefringent. As the white light travels through the cellophane and splits between two planes, the ordinary waves travel faster than the extraordinary waves. The waves, traveling at different speeds through different thicknesses of cellophane, produce a multitude of colors. The interference among waves creates the shifting boundaries of these colors.

Viewing the cellophane through a pair of polarized filters allows you to see these patterns more clearly.

Observe Polarized Light in a Crystal Solution

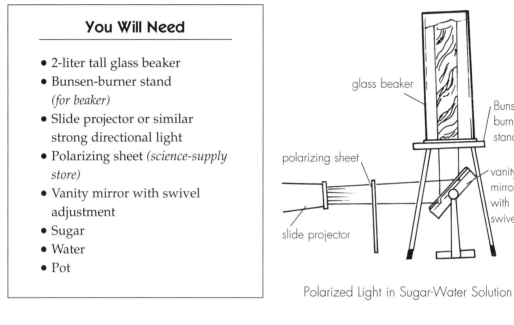

glass beaker

Bunsen-burner stand

polarizing sheet

vanity mirror with swivel

slide projector

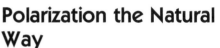

Polarized Light in Sugar-Water Solution

This project shows you how a simple sugar syrup can split white light into multiple refraction planes for a spectacularly colorful result.

The Motion of Light

The concept of light waves' traveling in planes might seem unusual at first, but think of the wavy motion of a taut rope. If you hold one end of the rope and shake it up and down, a wave travels through the rope that reflects the up-and-down shaking of your hand. If you shake the rope from side to side, the wave travels from side to side. Although both waves travel in straight lines, the plane of each wave is different, reflecting the motion of your hand.

Light waves behave very similarly. Although they travel in straight lines, each light wave moves along a specific plane that depends upon the vibrational direction (moving hand) of the original electron.

Polarization the Natural Way

The term *polarization* refers to light that has been filtered so that light waves traveling only along specific planes may pass through. The light is sent through a polarizing filter made from the same material used in non-glare sunglasses. Although high-grade polarizing filters are synthetic, some natural materials have the same effect. A certain class of noncubic crystals, called birefringent crystals, can filter light that passes through them into multiple planes. Since each plane affects the speed of the light wave, the light emerges from birefringent crystals in various colors. As this project will show, certain materials dissolved in a solution can have the same effect.

Polarizing filters are used in pairs so that the light travels through one filter and is observed through the other filter. The first filter is called the polarizer, and the second filter is called the analyzer. The object being examined is placed between the polarizer and analyzer. By shifting the position of the analyzer relative to the polarizer, various planes of light waves can be studied as they pass through the object.

Procedure

1. Heat 2 quarts (about 1 L) of water to boiling in a pot. Turn off the heat, and add sugar to the water until no more sugar dissolves. Allow the sugar-water solution to cool to room temperature.

2. Fill the beaker to the top with the sugar-water solution. Dispose of the excess solution.

3. Place the beaker on the stand, and put the mirror directly under the beaker. Swivel the mirror to a 45-degree angle.

4. Position the slide projector 18 inches (45 cm) from the mirror so that the beam of light hits the mirror and reflects up through the bottom of the beaker into the sugar solution. Adjust the mirror if necessary. You should have a column of light traveling up through the solution.

5. Hold the polarizing sheet between the slide projector and mirror, and slowly rotate the sheet while observing the column of light in the sugar solution. Record your observations.

Note: If possible, mount the polarizing sheet on a rotor similar to those used for Christmas-tree illumination.

Result

The column displays swirling colors. When you rotate the polarizing sheet, the colors rotate in barber-pole fashion around the central axis of the beam.

Explanation

The sugar solution simulates the polarizing effect of a birefringent crystal. It also functions as the analyzer part of the polarizer-analyzer pair. Continually in motion, the molecules of sugar polarize the white light in ever-shifting planes or vectors. As each vector shifts, it affects the speed of the light, and changes its color.

Did You Know?

Polarizing filters can tell scientists many things about a material because polarized light reveals details about a material's composition that ordinary light would not. When examined under polarized light, some types of glass reveal strain patterns. These wavy patterns show that the glass has been strengthened by rapid heating and cooling.

Three-Mirror Retroreflector

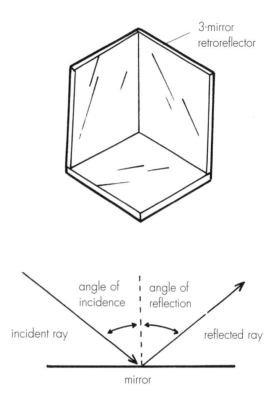

3-mirror retroreflector

You Will Need

- 3 small square mirrors, same size
- Low-power laser pointer (wavelength 630–680 nm)
- Masking tape
- Smoke medium, such as incense or burning punk
- White cardboard

In physics, the law of reflection states that light will always reflect at an angle identical to the angle of its source. This means that when a light beam strikes a surface and reflects, its angle of reflection will always equal its angle of incidence. These angles are measured against an imaginary line, called the normal, perpendicular to the reflecting plane. As this project demonstrates, the law of reflection allows scientists to easily predict, adjust, and correct—or retroreflect—-a trajectory of light when necessary.

angle of incidence | angle of reflection

incident ray | reflected ray

mirror

Observing Light Trajectory

Procedure

1. Tape the three mirrors together so that they form a half-cube.

2. Observe your reflection in the mirrors from various angles.

3. With one hand, point the laser at any one of the three mirrors. Hold the cardboard behind the laser with the other hand, and note where the reflected beam appears on the cardboard.

CAUTION: Never point a laser directly at your eyes, and do not stand in the path of the reflected laser beam.

4. Place a smoking medium next to the mirrors and darken the room.

5. Repeat step #3, this time observing the trajectory of the laser beam.

Result

When you look at your reflection in the mirror, your face appears in the corner where the three mirrors join. No matter where you move, your reflection always appears in the same corner. When you point the laser at the mirror, the beam always reflects back along a parallel line. This remains true no matter at which of the three mirrors you aim the laser.

Explanation

Since the mirrors are arranged in three mutually perpendicular planes, the light is "corrected" through multiple reflections. This means that the angle of reflection created by the first mirror will always be cancelled out by a second mirror and the light sent back along a path parallel to the original angle of incidence. This is how the image of your face, caught in three mirrors and reflected at three different angles, is straightened out and returned in parallel lines. Similarly, the laser beam reflects in a path parallel to its original trajectory.

Total Internal Reflection of Laser Light in Water

This project demonstrates the basic optical principle of total internal reflection, which states that a beam of light must reflect at an angle smaller than the critical angle of a medium in order to escape the medium. The laser in water also makes a pretty good light show!

Procedure

1. Spray-paint one side of the screen white and allow the paint to dry.

2. Loosen the label from the plastic bottle by soaking the bottle in warm soapy water. Carefully peel the label from the bottle, making sure that you leave no glue residue behind.

3. Drill a $\frac{1}{16}$-inch (1.5-mm) hole in the side of the bottle near the bottom.

4. Use the craft knife to pare down the cork until it fits snugly into the hole.

5. Fill the bottle with water and place it cork-forward at the edge of the higher table.

6. Place the aquarium lengthwise on the lower table, and move the table so that it's no more than 6 inches (15 cm) from the higher table.

7. Lean the screen, painted side up, at a 45-degree angle inside the aquarium. Don't worry if the top of the screen pokes out of the aquarium.

8. Put the laser pointer directly behind the bottle, and aim the beam through the water so that the beam is centered on the cork. You may have to prop the laser up on a book for this to work.

9. Without disturbing the alignment of the laser light on the cork, remove the cork and observe the stream of water as it hits the white screen in the aquarium. The effect is heightened if you lower the lights.

Result

The stream of water luminesces slightly, and a bright spot of laser light appears at the point where the stream hits the screen.

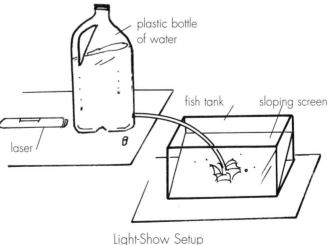

Light-Show Setup

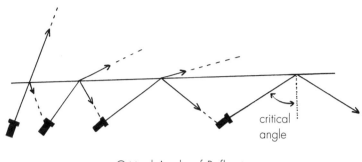

Critical Angle of Reflection
(flashlight underwater)

Explanation

The laser light is caught within the stream of water because the beam reflects at an angle greater than the *critical angle* it would need to escape the water. Critical angle is an important concept in physics. It means that when light travels through a medium—solid, liquid, gas—at an angle greater than the critical angle for that medium, the light can't escape the medium and remains in a state of total internal reflection. The drawing shows how an underwater beam of light must have an angle smaller than the critical angle of water in order to leave the water. The critical angle is measured from an imaginary line called the normal. Each medium has its own unique critical angle.

For water, it's 48 degrees from the normal; for diamonds it's 24 degrees—smaller than for any other known substance.

As for the stream of water, you can see from the diagram that the laser light is carried along the stream through of a series of total internal reflections. Each angle of reflection is greater than the critical angle of 48 degrees for water, and so the light remains inside the water.

Did You Know?

Scientists in the optics industry have developed special glasslike materials. Rods and threads made of this special material can carry light as a hose carries water. Very little of the light escapes from the sides of these optic fibers, and the light may be "pumped" hundreds of miles. Someday our homes may be lighted with optic fibers instead of lamps in every room. A single source of low-energy light in your basement will be piped to all the rooms of your house.

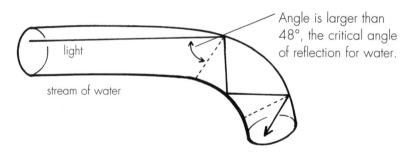

Testing the Angle of Reflection for Water

Change the Refractive Index of Wool

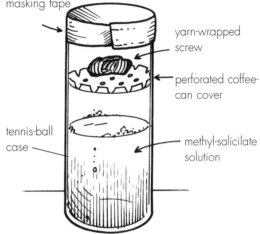

Changing the Refractive Index of Wool

You Will Need

- Wool yarn
- Tennis-ball can (cylindrical with cap)
- Methyl salicylate *(science-supply store)*
- Small screw
- Plastic lid from a 13-ounce (about 365-g) coffee can
- Sharp nail
- Masking tape
- Ruler
- Scissors

If you tried the "Birefringence in a Sheet of Cellophane" project, you saw how materials with identical light-bending qualities can, when combined, create contrasting effects. This project demonstrates how two very different materials can become optically identical.

Procedure

1. Use the ruler to measure the diameter of the opening of the tennis-ball can. Cut the coffee-can cover into a circle with a diameter 1½ inches (3.75 cm) wider than the can's opening.

2. Poke six holes in the coffee-can cover with the nail, and use the scissors to cut the edge of the cover into the pattern shown in the illustration.

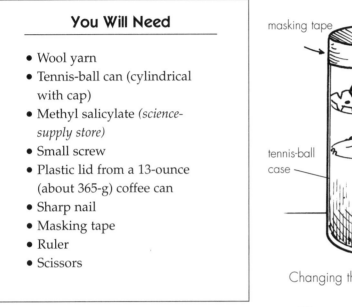

Coffee-Can Cover

3. Wrap enough wool yarn around the small screw to completely cover it.

4. Fill the tennis-ball can to the ¼ mark with methyl salicylate.

5. Push the coffee-can cover into the tennis-ball can so that the flanges of the cover bend up against the walls of the case. Keep the cover level as you push it down to about 3 inches (7.5 cm) of the top.

6. Place the wool-wrapped screw on top of the cover, and place the cap on the tennis-ball can. Secure the cap with a strip of masking tape wrapped around the case from top to bottom.

7. Slowly invert the tennis-ball can so that the methyl salicylate flows through the holes in the cover and saturates the wool. Record your observations.

8. Turn the tennis-ball can right side up again so that the methyl salicylate flows out of the wool. Record your observations.

Result

As the wool yarn absorbs the methyl salicylate, the wool becomes glasslike and transparent, clearly revealing the screw hidden inside. (This effect will be less dramatic if you use brightly colored wool.) As the methyl salicylate drains from the wool, the wool becomes opaque again.

Explanation

When saturated, the fibers of wool have the identical light-bending properties of the methyl salicylate. This means that both wool and methyl salicylate have the same refractive index as long as the wool remains saturated.

The term *refractive index* refers to the bending of light as it passes from the air into a solid, liquid, or gaseous medium. Since the index depends on the density (and temperature) of the medium, a solid may have the same refractive index as a liquid, and a liquid may share an identical refractive index with a gas. In this case, the refractive indices of methyl salicylate and saturated wool are so similar that it's difficult to distinguish the outline of wool fibers while they are suspended in the solution.

Compare Refractive Indices of Three Substances

You Will Need

- 2 small scientific beakers, straight sides
- 2 glass microscope slides
- Grease pencil
- Mineral oil
- Water

Although it's usually possible to recognize an ice cube in water, this project will show that certain transparent materials become practically invisible when combined.

Procedure

1. Using a grease pencil, on one of the microscope slides write OIL. On the other slide write WATER.

2. Fill one of the glass beakers to the halfway mark with mineral oil. Fill the other glass beaker to the same level with water.

3. Place the OIL slide in the mineral-oil beaker. Place the WATER slide in the water beaker. Record what you see.

4. Move the desk lamp around the beakers and adjust the angle of the lamp. Record additional observations.

Result

In the beaker containing the oil, the glass slide seems to disappear, making the word OIL appear suspended in the liquid. In the beaker containing water, the glass slide is clearly visible.

Explanation

Light travels through glass and water at different angles, but it travels through oil and water at nearly the same angle. Glass and water have different refractive indices, while glass and oil have similar indices. The term *refractive index* refers to the bending of light as it passes from the air into a solid, liquid, or gaseous medium. The index is affected by both the density of the medium and its temperature. Heating the oil would give it a refractive index much closer to that of water, as would substituting Plexiglas rods for the glass ones.

As you can see, a solid can have the same refractive index as a liquid. Since at room temperature the refractive indices of glass and mineral oil are so similar, it's very difficult to distinguish the boundaries of the glass slide when it's submerged in the oil. As far as the traveling photons of light are concerned, both glass and oil are the same substance.

Mechanics & Motion

The Components of Force

You Will Need

- Child-size skateboard
- DC electric motor *(science-supply store)**
- Plastic propeller attachment
- Two 5-foot (1.5-m) insulated wires in different colors
- 1½ × 1½ × 4-inch wooden dowel *(large dowel)*
- Two ½ × ½ × 1½-inch wooden dowels *(small dowels)*
- 1 ½ × 4-inch piece of plywood
- Molly bolt (just the screw part)
- 9-volt batteries
- 2 metal washers
- Cardboard
- Plastic protractor
- White glue
- Drill
- Screwdriver
- Wood stapler
- Masking tape
- Skill saw
- Stopwatch
- Yardstick or meterstick

Fan-Motor Skateboard

This propeller-driven skateboard demonstrates the combined effect of forward and lateral forces on a moving object.

Procedure

1. Use the skill saw to carefully remove the straight-ruler section of the protractor, leaving only the degree arc. Then use the saw to cut a V-shape in one end of the large square dowel.

2. Turn the dowel upside down, and drill a hole in the center of the flat end. The hole should be just large enough to contain the molly bolt.

3. Drill a hole at the center of the plywood piece, and with a little glue attach a smaller dowel to each end of the piece, making a kind of tray.

4. Attach the tray to the dowel with the molly bolt, placing a metal washer between the dowel and the tray's surface and between the tray bottom and screw head (see illustration). You should be able to pivot the dowel against the tray.

Tray-and-Dowel Assembly

5. Turn the dowel so that it rests on its tray. Place the electric motor in the V-shape you cut earlier. Drape a strip of tape over the

*The DC electric motor—6v/600 mA, 5500 rpm—from Edmund Scientific, #CR53–512, works well. www.edmundscientific.com

top of the motor and stick the ends of the tape to the sides of the dowel. If the tape begins to peel, staple it to the dowel with the wood stapler. Attach the plastic propeller to the motor shaft.

Note: Depending on the size of the propeller's center hole, you may have to use some epoxy cement to secure the propeller to the nut on the motor's axle.

6. Cut a 1½ × 3½-inch (3.75 × 8.75-cm) arrow from the cardboard. Make a small fold on the flat side of the arrow, and glue the fold to the dowel on the side opposite the propeller.

7. Place the entire fan—assembly-fan, motor, dowel, and tray—at the back of the skateboard. The tray should sit at a right angle to the propeller.

8. Place the protractor at the arrow side of the fan assembly so that the arc curves around the dowel. Adjust the position of the protractor so that the arrow clearly indicates a degree mark. Then tape down the ends of the protractor.

9. Twist the different-colored wires together, leaving the ends loosely twisted. Attach one end of each colored wire to the terminal wires of the motor. Tape one colored wire to the negative terminal of the battery and the other colored wire to the positive terminal.

10. Place the skateboard on a smooth, level surface and put the yardstick next to it. Pivot the fan assembly so that the arrow points to 0 degrees on the protractor.

11. Holding the battery, stand away from the skateboard and touch the end of the wire to the positive pole, starting the motor.

Allow the skateboard to roll forward for 5 seconds (time it with the stopwatch) and then disconnect the wire.

12. Measure the distance the skateboard traveled in 5 seconds with the fan set at 0 degrees.

13. Turn the fan to 45 degrees, and then to 90 degrees, and repeat step #12.

Result

The skateboard's acceleration and speed diminish in proportion to the angle of the fan. At 0 (zero) degrees, the fan produces maximum forward force on the skateboard, resulting in the highest rate of acceleration and speed. At 45 degrees, the fan produces both a forward and lateral force on the skateboard, so that the skateboard will accelerate at only half the rate and travel at half the speed than when the fan was at 0 degrees. At 90 degrees, the fan produces no forward force on the skateboard, only a lateral force, so the skateboard doesn't move at all.

Explanation

Think of the forward and lateral forces acting on the skateboard as two force directions, or vectors. These vectors always act in combination, and their combination determines the acceleration, speed, and final trajectory path of the skateboard. Since the wheels of the skateboard are fixed forward, the skateboard always travels in a straight line. This means that the trajectory of the skateboard can't change to reflect the interaction of forward and lateral vectors, and this interaction is reflected solely in the skateboard's acceleration and speed.

A Short Ride with a Helium Balloon

You Will Need

- Balloon filled with helium
- Balloon you blow up (same size as helium balloon)
- Yardstick or meterstick
- Tape
- Slow-moving vehicle

This project requires the forward motion of a closed space. The passenger seat of a slow-moving car will do nicely. Although the behavior of the balloons will seem puzzling at first, they clearly demonstrate the force of acceleration on gases of different densities.

Procedure

1. Find two round balloons. Fill one with helium (party-supply stores will do this) and, using your own breath, blow up the other to about the same size.

2. Tape the tied end of each balloon to an end of the yardstick. Use enough tape so that the balloons stand upright but can bob freely.

3. Take your balloons and yardstick into the car, and place the yardstick in your lap so that a balloon sticks out on either side.

4. At the count of three, ask the driver to start moving forward. Closely watch both balloons for about 5 seconds; then have the driver stop.

5. Have the driver move the car in reverse. Watch the balloons; record your observations.

Result

When the car moves forward, the breath-inflated balloon jerks backwards while the helium-inflated balloon jerks forward in the direction of movement. When the car moves backwards, the motions of the balloons reverse.

Explanation

An object at rest tends to remain at rest, and this is called the force of inertia. It might seem unusual to think of inertia as a force, but consider this: when the car begins to move, inertia tries to prevent everything inside the car from moving with it. Your body begins to move only because the car seat pushes forward on you.

It's the same with the air in the car. The air moves forward only because it's pushed by the back wall. But since the air in the front of the car has nothing to push against it but the air in the back of the car, a momentary collision of air masses—back against front—occurs. As the air in back moves forward, it pushes against the air in front and sends it backward. This colliding and mixing continues until both front and back air are traveling at the same speed—the speed of the moving car.

The balloons behave differently during this clash of air masses because the helium-filled balloon is much lighter than the balloon you inflated with carbon dioxide from your breath. Helium is also much lighter than the surrounding air in the car, while carbon dioxide is heavier. As the faster-moving air in the back pushes forward against the slower-moving air in the front, it pushes the lighter-than-air helium balloon with it. The heavier carbon-dioxide balloon, unaffected by the moving air, retains its inertia and lurches forward only as a result of being pulled by the moving yardstick.

The Physics of a Geyser Eruption

You Will Need

- Club soda in a bottle with a plastic screw cap
- 4½-inch (about 11-cm) -diameter plastic funnel
- 3 feet (90 cm) of ³/₁₆-inch (about 5-mm) -diameter rubber tubing
- Circular 12-inch-diameter piece of plywood (base)
- 1 × 6-inch wooden dowel
- Modeling clay
- 1¾-inch screws
- 1¼-inch screws
- Large paper clip
- Rubber cement
- Saw
- Drill with ⁵/₁₆-inch bit

The physical forces that lead to the eruption of a geyser can be easily demonstrated in this project. The action of geysers provided early 19th century engineers with important clues that the power of steam could be harnessed and used in industry.

Procedure

1. Drill a hole in the center of the plywood base. Make sure the hole is large enough for the rubber tubing.

2. Cut the dowel into three 2-inch (5-cm) pieces.

3. Space the dowels evenly along the edge of the circular base. Screw each dowel to the base, turning the base into a miniature table.

4. Position the funnel in the center of the base so that its spout aligns with the hole you drilled. Use a few 1¼-inch screws along the edge of the funnel to secure it in place.

5. Mold clay around the funnel, creating a realistic geyser cone. Look at pictures of Old Faithful or similar famous geyser sites to get a feel for the topography around a geyser.

6. Remove the plastic cap from the club-soda bottle. While holding the cap with pliers against a firm surface, carefully drill a hole in the center of the cap.

7. Place the cap back on the bottle and insert 3 inches (7.5 cm) of plastic tubing into the hole. Brush some rubber cement around the tubing where it enters the hole to make a watertight seal.

8. Insert the other end of the tubing through the hole in the bottom of the base and up through the funnel so that the tip of the tubing protrudes slightly from the funnel spout.

9. Position the bottle about 1 foot (30 cm) lower than the base. At the middle point, using a large paper clip or your finger, pinch the tubing closed.

10. With one hand still pinching the tubing, shake the club soda so that you release the carbon-dioxide gases.

11. Release the tube and stand back.

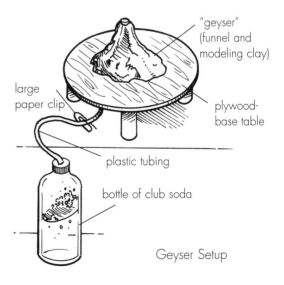

Geyser Setup

"geyser" (funnel and modeling clay)

large paper clip

plywood-base table

plastic tubing

bottle of club soda

Result

Liquid and vapor shoot from your geyser, gradually calming down and stopping.

Explanation

While your model only simulates the heat-generated action of a real geyser, it accurately demonstrates the force of rising pressure on a narrow column of water. In nature, geyser eruptions occur at the top of a long column of water that may extend deep into the earth. Due to geothermal heating, the temperature at the bottom of the water column increases until the water becomes hot enough to turn into steam. But steam is prevented from forming because of the weight of the water column above. After a while, the temperature of the water rises to the point where steam starts to form anyway. Since water expands as it turns into less dense steam, the column is pushed to the surface where it's projected with great force, followed by a plume of steam. Since the escaping water and steam release pressure in the column, the steam condenses into liquid water again and flows back down into the column, ready for the next geyser eruption.

When you shook the bottle of club soda, you provided enough "heat" energy to the carbon-dioxide molecules to allow them to leave the liquid portion of the soda and return to their more natural gaseous state. This carbon-dioxide "steam" accumulated in the closed, air-filled space above the soda. Since air took up much of this space to begin with, and since the bubbles of carbon dioxide continued to escape even after you finished shaking, the closed chamber became pressurized. Pinching the tube represents the weight of liquid water above the pressure. When you unpinched the tube, you allowed the carbon-dioxide gas to escape, followed with a spray of gas and soda.

The Trebuchet

You Will Need

- 10 · 24-inch plywood (*platform*)
- Two 1 · 4 · 18-inch wood pieces (*braces*)
- Four 1 · 2 · 15-inch wood pieces (*struts*)
- Two 1 · 2 · 13½-inch wood pieces (*posts*)
- ¼ · 1¼ · 26¼-inch wood piece (*catapult*)
- ⁵⁄₁₆ · 13½-inch wooden dowel
- Two 1-inch-diameter wooden-ball drawer-pulls
- 2¾ · 4½-inch cloth (*sling*)
- 34 inches (85 cm) strong string
- 3¾ · 11-inch (9.4 × 27.5-cm) foam board
- 2-liter plastic liquid-detergent bottle (*weight basket*)
- Coil of steel wire or something similar (*for weight*)
- Grape (*ammunition*)
- 1 brass fastener
- Small paper clip
- 4 ball-bearing wheel casters with screws
- 1¼-inch wood nails
- 1¼-inch wire-brad nails
- 1¾-inch screw
- 1¼-inch screw
- Three ⁵⁄₁₆-inch eye screws
- Two ¹¹⁄₁₆-inch linoleum nails
- Two ⁵⁄₁₆-inch washers
- Drill with ⁵⁄₃₂-, ¹⁄₁₆-, and ⁵⁄₁₆-inch bits
- Miter saw
- Screwdriver
- Wire cutters
- Pliers
- Carpenter's glue
- White glue
- Epoxy cement
- Craft knife

The trebuchet was an ingenious catapult weapon that changed the course of European warfare in the 13th century. It was used by Edward I of England to penetrate fortresses at the border of Scotland. So successful was the trebuchet at destroying castles that it was dreaded for over 200 years until the powder-fired cannon replaced it. The key to the trebuchet's success was its power, and as this working model will show, the power of the trebuchet came from its efficient use of force and momentum.

A photo of the trebuchet is on the book cover.

Platform & Struts

Procedure

1. Use the miter saw to cut the left ends of the 18-inch wood pieces (braces) at a 60-degree angle. Reverse the pieces and cut the opposite ends at 60 degrees. The angles of the edges should mirror each other.

2. Pre-drill holes with the ⁵⁄₁₆-inch bit, then use the 1¾-inch screws to attach the long sides of the braces to the long edges of the plywood platform. Notice from the drawing that the braces touch only one end of the platform and aren't centered.

3. Turn the platform over and screw a wheel caster to each corner.

4. Turn the platform right side up. Nail a post—use the 1 × 2 × 13½-inch wood piece—to the center of each brace. Use the 1½-inch nails.

5. Cut the ends of each of the four struts at a 30-degree angle. Place the struts at opposite sides of the posts so that they "lean" toward the center, and attach each strut to the brace and post with nails. Use a wire-brad nail to attach the top of each strut to the top of the post. You can also reinforce this joint with a little bit of carpenter's glue.

6. At the top of each post, drill a ⅟₁₆-inch hole. Insert a screw eye into each hole.

7. If you plan to finish your trebuchet, paint the platform assembly before continuing. When dry, position and glue the foam board so that it's centered between the post and the strut closest to the long end of the platform.

Catapult & Sling

Procedure

1. Cut one corner from the end of the 26¼-inch piece of wood for the catapult.

2. Carefully hammer a brad nail into this corner so that about ¼ inch (0.62 cm) of it sticks out. Cut off the end of the nail with the wire cutter.

3. From the same end, measure 2¾ inches (6.8 cm) along the bottom of the catapult and drill a ⅟₁₆-inch hole in the edge. Insert an eye screw into this hole.

4. Measure 8¾ inches (22 cm) from the opposite end of the catapult and drill a hole in the center of the arm using the ⁵⁄₁₆-inch bit. Measure ¼ inch (0.62 cm) from the same end and drill another hole.

5. Cut the dowel into two pieces, 11½ inches and 2 inches. At each end of the 2-inch (5-cm) piece, carefully drill and insert a linoleum nail so that about ¼ inch (0.62 cm) of it sticks out. These nails will act as pivots for the weight basket.

6. Insert the smaller piece into the hole closest to the end of the catapult and the larger piece into the remaining hole. Secure each piece with a little glue and allow the entire catapult assemble to dry overnight.

7. Use the craft knife or scissors to cut off the bottom of the detergent bottle and shape it into a basket. At the top of each basket handle, punch a hole just large enough to fit over the linoleum nail heads.

8. Make a hole on each narrow side of the cloth sling. Cut a 3-inch (7.5-cm) and 7-inch (17.5-cm) piece of string and knot one end of each piece to each of the holes.

9. At the free end of the 7-inch (17.5-cm) string, tie a ⁵⁄₁₆-inch washer, then loop the washer over the corner nail on the catapult. Tie the free end of the 3-inch (7.5-cm) piece to the eye screw on the catapult.

10. Use the ⁵⁄₁₆-inch drill bit to enlarge the holes on the wooden-ball drawer-pulls (or ornaments). Hold each ball tightly with pliers before attempting to drill. Make sure the balls fit snugly over the ends of the long dowel but can also be removed.

11. Attach the finished catapult by inserting the ends of the long dowel into the eye screws at the top of the posts. Attach the wooden balls to the ends of the dowels to lock the catapult in place. Attach the basket to the short piece of dowel.

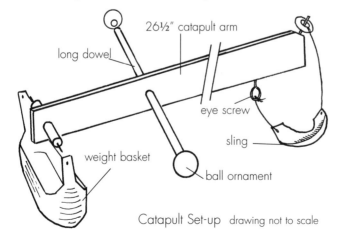

26½" catapult arm

long dowel

eye screw

weight basket

sling

ball ornament

Catapult Set-up   drawing not to scale

12. Tilt the catapult so that the long end touches the platform. At a point on the platform directly below the eye screw, drill a hole and partially insert a 1¼-inch screw. Make sure the hole is large enough to countersink the screw.

13. Cut a 2½-inch (6.2-cm) piece of string. Tie one end to the other ⁵⁄₁₆-inch washer and the other end to the partially inserted screw on the platform. Tighten the screw.

14. Tie one end of the remaining string to the brass fastener. This is the trigger string.

Loading, Cocking & Firing

Procedure

1. Tip the long end of the catapult to the platform. Insert the grape into the sling, fold the sling, and pull it taut on the foam board. Make sure that the washer on the long piece of string attaches to the wire brad at the tip of the catapult.

2. Hold the washer at the end of the platform-attached string against the eye screw of the catapult. Insert the brass fastener of the trigger spring through both washer and eye screw. Bend the prongs of the fastener to keep it from slipping out.

3. Place the wire coil in the basket, and allow the weight to pull the catapult down a few inches so that the trigger strings become taut.

4. Position your trebuchet so that nothing impedes the path of the grape when it flies through the air. Hold the end of the trigger string and move to the side of the catapult.

5. When you're ready to fire, jerk the trigger string, releasing the brass fastener. Driven by the weight in the basket, the catapult will swing and hurl the grape. The projectile path of the grape can be changed by changing the length of the strings on the sling. Longer strings create higher, steeper paths, and shorter strings allow lower, longer paths.

Mechanical Motion of the Trebuchet

The trebuchet works by applying force to a pendulum while maximizing the pendulum's momentum. The dropping weight

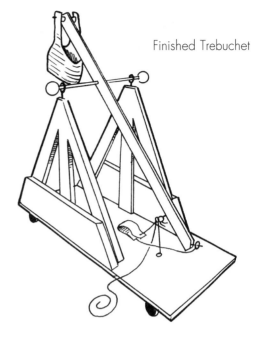

Finished Trebuchet

provides the force, while the swinging basket, length of sling, and wheeled platform all work together to create optimal energy in the swing.

When you pull the trigger string and allow the weight to drop, the swing of the catapult arm moves the platform slightly forward on its wheels. This forward motion allows the weighted end of the arm to fall farther down in its arc, increasing the arm's momentum. Since the basket pivots against the arm, the weight also falls farther in its arc, giving the swing an additional boost. At the opposite end of the arm, the thread holding the grape becomes taut, extending the length of the swinging arm and increasing momentum even further.

You can adjust each of these components to test its effect on cumulative momentum (for example, by shortening the length of the sling as mentioned). Also, securing the platform so that it can't roll forward will result in a dissipation of the swing's energy as the platform pitches forward. Tightening the screws of the weighted basket will keep the weight from dropping as far, decreasing momentum. And finally, adding less weight to the basket results in less force applied to the arm.

Discover Minimal Surface Areas

You Will Need

- 4-inch square plywood
- 4 × 4 × 4-inch plywood (equilateral-triangle shape)
- Spool of medium-gauge copper wire
- Spool of narrow-gauge copper wire
- Laundry basin
- Plastic gallon (or 4-L) jug
- Measuring cup
- Dishwashing liquid detergent
- Corn syrup
- Water

This project demonstrates a fail-proof method for finding the minimal surface area of any geometric shape—soap film! The elastic surface tension of soap will trace out surprising surfaces on familiar geometric shapes.

Procedure

1. Wrap the medium-gauge copper wire around the perimeter of the plywood square. Where the wire meets itself, cut off the excess. Press the wire tightly against the corners of the square, and carefully slip the wire from the plywood so that you have a perfect square traced in the wire. Repeat this procedure to make three more wire squares.

2. Wrap a second length of medium-gauge wire around the perimeter of the plywood triangle, clipping off the excess.

Press the wire tightly against the corners and remove the wire triangle from the plywood. Make two more wire triangles this way.

3. Use the narrow wire to attach the 4 wire squares together, making a 6-sided cube. Attach the 3 wire triangles together to make a 4-sided shape called a tetrahedron. Attach a 12-inch (30-cm) length of medium-gauge wire to a corner of both the cube and tetrahedron so that you have two dipping wands.

4. Fill the laundry basin with water, using the gallon jugs. Keep track of how many gallons of water you used, and add 1 cup (240 ml) of laundry detergent and ½ cup (120 ml) of corn syrup for each gallon (3.8 L) of water. Stir the water thoroughly.

5. Dip the cube wand in the water and remove it. Examine the soap film along the edges and surfaces of the wire cube.

6. Dip the tetrahedron wand into the water and examine it. Examine the soap film.

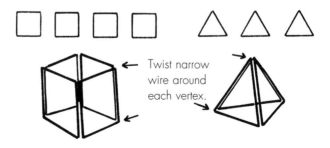

Attach wire squares together to make a cube.

Attach wire triangles together to make a tetrahedron.

Result

Rather than fill in the empty walls, or faces, of the cube and tetrahedron, the film creates new surfaces between the faces that join at the center of each shape. These surfaces, as complex as they may seem, actually define the minimal surface area for both a cube and a tetrahedron.

Explanation

The Surface Tension of Water: The mutual attraction of hydrogen molecules gives water a kind of internal "stickiness," and this stickiness shows as surface tension where the water meets the air. Adding soap to water decreases surface tension by two-thirds. This means that soap allows you to "stretch" water over a wider area, like the wires of your bubble wands. The important feature of stretched water is that it will always contract into the smallest possible area.

This is why bubbles are so important to physicists—they have the "intelligence" to create shapes that combine volume and surface area in the most efficient way possible. The simplest example of this is the sphere. The soap film that formed around your cube and tetrahedron translated these geometric forms into their most surface-volume efficient counterparts.

Shape	Number of Sides	Volume	Surface Area
Tetrahedron	4	1 cubic inch	7.21 sq. inches
Cube	6	1 cubic inch	6 sq. inches
Octahedron	8	1 cubic inch	5.72 sq. inches
Dodecahedron	12	1 cubic inch	5.32 sq. inches
Icosahedron	20	1 cubic inch	5.15 sq. inches
Sphere	Infinite	1 cubic inch	4.84 sq. inches

Adjust Surface Tension with a Bar of Soap

You Will Need

- 2 small bars of floating soap (courtesy-size hotel soap is best)
- White ceramic casserole plate
- Craft knife
- Sharp pencil
- Finely ground pepper
- Water

This project demonstrates how the surface tension of water can be affected by introducing an inorganic soluble substance, namely soap.

Procedure

1. Use the craft knife to cut both soap bars in half. Use a little water on your fingertip to round out the corners.

2. Fill the casserole dish with cool water and sprinkle pepper in the water until you have a light coating of pepper floating on the surface.

3. Carefully insert the point of the sharpened pencil into one of the half bars of soap. Push the pencil in just far enough so that you can lift the soap but easily shake it free.

4. Holding the pencil, slowly lower the soap into the water until its flat side just makes contact with the water's surface. Watch the pepper.

5. Give the pencil a slight downward shake so that the soap breaks free. Observe the movement of the soap in the water.

6. Empty the soap and water from the casserole dish, and thoroughly rinse and dry the dish so that no soap residue remains. Refill the dish with water and sprinkle pepper as before.

7. Cut one end of the second half bar of soap into an arrow. Insert the pencil point into the soap and lower the soap into the water, watching the pepper.

8. Shake the soap free, observe its movement, and then rinse out the casserole dish.

9. Cut the remaining half bars of soap into a circle and jagged shape. Use a little water on your fingertip to smooth out the edges of the circle. Repeat steps #2–6 with these shapes.

Result

When the rectangular soap bar is placed in the water, the floating pepper moves away from all edges, but farther away from the corners. When the bar is released in the water, it doesn't move appreciably in any direction.

When the arrow-shaped bar is placed in the water, the pepper pulls sharply away from the point of the arrow. When the soap is released, it moves in a direction opposite the arrow.

When the circular bar of soap is placed in the water, the pepper retreats uniformly from the circle's edge, forming a "border" of clear water around the soap that slowly expands. When the soap is released, it doesn't move in any direction.

When the jagged soap is placed in the water, the pepper pulls sharply back from every point. When the soap is released, it moves first in one direction and then in another direction.

Explanation

Every molecule in water attracts its neighbor. This is because the two hydrogen atoms, attached to one side of an H_2O molecule, attract the single oxygen atom of another molecule. This mutual attraction of molecules in water is called hydrogen bonding. To strengthen the bond, hydrogen atoms are positively charged while oxygen atoms are negatively charged.

When water is in the liquid state, its molecules have too much energy to become locked in a fixed position, and so slide around one another. Still, the bonding of molecules gives water a kind of internal "stickiness," and this stickiness shows as surface tension where the water meets the air. Adding soap to water decreases surface tension dramatically. In your project, the molecules of soap, streaming out from various points along the edge of the bar, broke the surface tension of the water as traced by the movement of the pepper. The water's surface tension tore more quickly at the pointed edges of the soap. This is because more water comes into contact with soap, and the concentration of dissolving soap is highest at these points. Like the motion of a torn elastic sheet, the remaining surface tension on the opposite side of the point pulled the soap away from the tear. When the tear is uniform, as it was for the rectangular and circular soaps, each pulling force is counteracted by a pulling force in the opposite direction. This is why neither the rectangle nor circle moved.

Compare Static & Sliding Friction

You Will Need

- Two ¼ × 6 × 36-inch wood planks
- Two ⅛ × ⅛ × 36-inch balsa-wood strips
- Small wood block
- Thumbtacks
- 1 hinge with 4 screws
- Glue
- Medium-gauge sandpaper
- Clear plastic protractor
- Yardstick or meterstick
- Red felt-tip marking pen
- Epoxy glue
- Thumbtacks
- Testing materials: aluminum foil, cellophane, paper towel, wrapping tissue paper, terry cloth, newspaper, shiny magazine cover, plastic bag

Physicists and engineers study two states of friction: the state of static friction and the state of sliding friction. When the tires of your car grip the road and move you forward, static friction is at work. When you turn a corner too fast and begin to skid, sliding friction takes over. Static friction is stronger and allows irregular surfaces to lock together.

Sliding friction occurs when another force exceeds the limits of static friction so that irregular surfaces slip against one another. In this project, static friction keeps various materials from slipping down a ramp until the ramp is inclined far enough so that sliding friction takes over. Each material has its own static-friction threshold, which you'll measure in degrees.

Ramp Construction

Procedure

1. Sand one side of the ramp plank until the surface seems smooth and slippery. Place it, sanded side up, over the base plank.

2. Join the two planks with the hinge so that the ramp plank closes over the base plank like a book cover.

3. Apply a bead of glue to one side of each balsa-wood strip, and gently press the strips along the long edges of the ramp plank. The strips should form a fence, keeping the test materials from sliding off the plank.

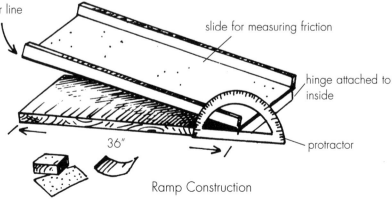

red indicator line

slide for measuring friction

hinge attached to inside

36"

protractor

Ramp Construction

4. Use the yardstick and red felt-tip marking pen to draw a straight line along the base of one fence. The red line will be an indicator line to show the degree of inclination through the protractor.

5. Attach the plastic protractor to the base plank so that the middle of the protractor falls directly where the two planks join. If your protractor has a convenient screw hole for this, use a small screw. If not, attach the protractor to the wood with a little epoxy glue.

6. Make sure the ramp plank moves easily against the protractor and that the red indicator line is clearly visible.

Static-Friction Test

Procedure

1. With the ramp plank flat against the base plank, place the wooden block at the unhinged end of the ramp plank. Slowly raise the ramp plank until the block begins to slide (it doesn't have to slide all the way to the bottom). Note the degree of inclination on the protractor and write it down. To validate your result, repeat this test four more times, each time noting the degree of inclination.

2. Wrap the block in a piece of aluminum foil. Keep the foil smooth and unwrinkled. Repeat step #1 and note the degree of inclination. Repeat the test four more times.

3. Continue the experiment by wrapping the block in cellophane, paper towel, fine-gauge sandpaper, tissue paper, terry cloth, newspaper, shiny magazine cover, and plastic bag. Use thumbtacks to fasten materials like sandpaper and terry cloth to the block. Repeat each test four times and record all results.

Result

If you made a list of your data, it might look like this:

Material	Ramp Angle (Degrees)
aluminum foil	10
shiny magazine cover	18
plastic bag	20
wood block	22
plastic wrap	24
newspaper	28
sandpaper (fine)	36
paper towel	39
sandpaper (medium)	42
sandpaper (coarse)	44
terry cloth	46
tissue paper	46

Explanation

The block provides a constant mass for each material you test. The block's shape ensures that the air resistance will also be a constant. This allows you to more clearly isolate the static-friction threshold for each material. In general, materials made from coarser fibers—newspaper, cloth, tissue—require a greater angle of inclination to slide. This is because the rough ends of the paper and cloth fibers, though microscopic, catch against the equally rough ends of the wood fibers. A metallic surface like aluminum foil and a plastic surface like cellophane slide much more easily against the wood because their surfaces are uniform. The same is true for the paste-treated paper of a magazine.

Conserve Angular Momentum

You Will Need

- Rotating stool or chair
- Two 1-pound (450-g) barbells
- Stopwatch
- 2 willing friends

This project requires two assistants, one of whom is willing to go for a short spin in a rotating chair. The result will be well worth the dizziness.

Procedure

1. Place your friend in the rotating chair and hand him a 1-pound (450-g) barbell for each hand. Have him sit straight with his arms hanging down over the sides of the chair.

2. Crouch down in front of your friend and push his knees so that he spins in one complete circle. Make sure you move away from your friend after the first push to avoid getting hit by the weights.

3. Have another friend, the timer, hold a stopwatch and call out "Spin!" at 2-second intervals. Follow the timer's direction so that every 2 seconds, you give your friend a push in his chair, setting up a fairly constant rate of rotation. Remember to step away from your friend after each and every push!

4. Instruct your friend to gradually move his arms out from his sides while you continue to push at 2-second intervals. Is the rate of your friend's rotation becoming more difficult to sustain?

5. Instruct your friend to hold his arms straight out from his body as you continue to push. Note if it takes more effort to keep your friend spinning.

6. Tell your friend to gradually lower his arms while you continue spinning him for a

little while. Note any change in your pushing efforts. Stop pushing and allow your friend to get over his dizziness before getting out of the chair.

Result

As your friend lifted his arms with the weights, you had to work harder to keep him spinning at a constant state of rotation. When his arms were fully outstretched, it took two pushes—one in front at his knees and the other behind at his hips—to complete one rotation. As he lowered his arms, the pushing required less work. In fact, you may have found that you could easily exceed the initial rate of rotation with little effort.

Explanation

Together, you and your friend were demonstrating conservation of angular momentum. Your friend, with his outstretched arms and weights, was behaving like a mechanical regulating device called a governor. You might recognize one of these devices as a small carousel-shaped object spinning on top of a rotary-motion machine like a generator. The governor ensures that the generator turbines do not speed up or slow down. How does it do this? The law of conservation of angular momentum states that as the radius of a rotating mass decreases, the velocity of rotation increases:

$$\text{Mass} \times \text{Radius} \times \text{Velocity} = \text{Constant Rate of Rotation}$$

In practical terms, this means that if a generator's turbine begins to spin too fast, it will spin the governor faster. The weights on the governor will swing outward, forcing the turbine to work harder to sustain its increased speed, and so it slows down. Conversely, if the turbine slows, the slower rotation of the governor will pull the weights closer, requiring less work from the turbine to speed up.

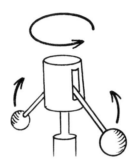

Simple Governor

Rubber-Band Heat Engine

You Will Need

- Fifteen 2-inch (5-cm) rubber bands
- 9-inch (about 22-cm) diameter embroidery hoop
- ½ × 4 ½ × 10¼-inch wood *(base)*
- ½ × 5½ × 12-inch wood *(shield)*
- ½ × 1½ × 12-inch wood *(post)*
- ½ × 5¾-inch wooden dowel
- Two 5⁄16-inch eye screws
- 1¼-inch wire-brad nails
- 1¾-inch screws
- 1¾-inch lock washer
- Two ½-inch wooden screw-hole buttons
- Drill with 5⁄16-inch bit
- Hammer
- Saw
- 2 pliers
- Craft knife
- Masking tape
- Carpenter's glue
- Strong desk lamp, with halogen bulb if possible

This project combines both chemistry and mechanical motion to create a unique device: the rubber-band heat engine. While not actually an engine powerful enough to be of any practical use, the engine will spin slowly with only the heat from a desk lamp to keep it going.

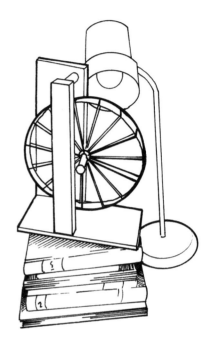

Wheel & Axle

Procedure

1. Hold the lock washer with the pliers. With the second pliers, pry the cut ends of the washer apart so that you can insert the rubber bands.

2. Loop the 15 rubber bands inside the washer; then use the pliers to close the washer gap.

3. Remove the inner ring of the embroidery hoop, and use the craft knife to carefully slice through the wood so that you gently pry open the ring.

4. Working on a flat surface, position the washer with rubber bands at the center of the ring. While gently prying the ring open, loop one end of a rubber band around the ring. Follow it with the remaining rubber bands, spacing them so that their tension is evenly distributed around the ring. When all

rubber bands have been attached to the ring, tape the ring closed.

5. Your wheel might look a little lopsided at this point. To balance it, you must space the rubber bands more evenly around the ring. Since a 9-inch (22.5-cm) hoop has a 30-inch (75-cm) circumference, each of the 15 rubber bands should be 2 inches (5 cm) apart.

6. When you've finished spacing the rubber bands, remove the tape from the ring. Gently pry the ends apart, apply a little glue, and push the ends together again. This will seal your ring closed.

7. Use the saw to cut a 2 ¾-inch (6.87-cm) piece from the dowel. Pre-drill holes, then gently tap a wire-brad nail into each end of the dowel so that each nail protrudes ¾ inch (about 1.8 cm). If necessary, use the pliers to make sure the nails protrude straight from the ends of the dowel.

8. Carefully push this axle piece through the lock washer containing the rubber bands. Avoid forcing the piece because you might snap a rubber band. Instead, carefully rock the axle until it sits at the exact center of the wheel.

9. Drill two shallow holes in the backs of the wooden screw-hole buttons. Insert a button over the protruding brads of the axle.

Wheel Mount

Procedure

1. Measure 6 inches (15 cm) from the end of the post and shield, and insert eye screws.

2. Attach the shield to the base with the 1¾-inch screws. Make sure the eye screw sits at the center of the base.

3. Attach the post to the base in the same way. Make sure the eye screw on the post lines up with the eye screw on the shield.

4. Use the remaining 3-inch (7.5-cm) piece of the wooden dowel as a top support between the post and the shield. Apply a little glue to each dowel end before inserting the dowel in position.

5. Assemble the engine by first removing the screw hole buttons from the ends of the axle brads. Then slide the brads into the eye screws of the post and shield. Replace the screw-hole buttons so that your engine looks finished.

6. Place a desk lamp in front of the shield so that only half of the wheel is illuminated. Wait about 5 minutes and record your observations.

Result

The wheel will begin to turn slowly. The rate of rotation will vary depending on how much heat the lamp throws and how carefully you've balanced the wheel. If your wheel fails to rotate after 5 minutes, check to make sure that the axle is centered and that the rubber bands are evenly spaced.

Explanation

When heated, rubber behaves differently than many other substances. Most substances expand when heated; rubber, however, contracts. In your heat engine, the portion of rubber band exposed to the light contracts as it absorbs the light's heat. This causes the rubber band to pull one edge of the wheel closer to the axle, which shifts the wheel's center of gravity. A shifted center of gravity means that the wheel is now "heavier" on one side and begins a partial rotation. This rotation, in turn, moves the heated rubber bands behind the shield where they can cool and moves other rubber bands into the light. This constant heating and cooling, resulting in a constantly shifting center of gravity, causes the wheel to rotate.

"Bounceability"

The physics of bouncing can provide important information to those who make bouncing balls their business, such as basketball players, handball players, tennis players, and the professionals who design their playing areas. This project requires two assistants, one of whom drops the ball while the other measures the bounce.

Procedure

1. Set up the stepladder on a firm, level surface. Straddle the broomstick across the middles of the two bottom steps of the stepladder, and tape the broomstick to the steps. Tape the yardstick to the broomstick vertically.

2. Inflate one of the beach balls and label it "A" with the permanent marker.

3. Cut the air hose from the other beach ball, making an opening no more than ½ inch (1.25 cm) in diameter. Label this beach ball "B."

4. Fill beach ball B with rice, using the funnel. Place a piece of masking tape over the opening to keep the rice inside the ball.

5. Take beach ball A to the top platform of the ladder. While your friend stands 3 feet (90 cm) in front of the ladder with his pencil and pad, carefully roll the ball from the platform so that it drops directly in front of the yardstick. In his book your friend should enter "1st drop: air" and record how high the ball bounced.

CAUTION: Never stand or sit on the top platform of a stepladder.

---

6. Take beach ball B to the top of the ladder and roll it off. Your friend should enter "2nd drop: rice" and record the height of the bounce.

7. Empty the air from beach ball A and fill it with water. To fill the ball completely, you'll have to pause and allow the air to escape as the water displaces it. Cap the hose tightly.

8. Empty the rice from beach ball B and replace it with puffed wheat, taping over the opening.

9. Bring each ball to the top of the ladder and roll it off. Your friend records "3rd drop: water" and "4th drop: puffed wheat," taking a bounce measurement for each.

10. Empty the water from ball A and replace it with shaving cream. To do this, hold the spout from the can into the inflation hose and carefully squirt the cream. Pause and gently knead the ball to allow air to escape and cream to settle. Cap the hose tightly.

11. Empty the puffed rice from ball B and replace it with sand, taping over the opening.

12. Bring each ball to the top of the platform and conduct two more bounce tests.

Result

Each ball showed a different bounce height depending on what the ball contained. The air-filled ball bounced the highest, followed by the shaving cream and puffed wheat. None of the balls filled with water, sand, or rice bounced at all.

Explanation

Two rebounding forces act upon a bouncing ball: (1) the force of the ball hitting a surface and (2) the force of the surface hitting a ball. The combined effect of these forces determines how high the ball bounces. Since the rebounding force of the ground remains constant, we can focus on comparing the rebounding forces among the various balls.

During impact on a hard surface, the skin of the ball dents. This denting depletes the ball's kinetic energy (energy of motion), since some of the energy goes into the dent, which must then "undent" to push the ball upward again. The less pressure inside the ball, the larger the dent and the more kinetic energy lost. This means less bounce. The more pressure, the smaller the dent and the more kinetic energy available for a higher bounce.

Only air provided enough pressure to minimize the ball's denting and maximize its kinetic energy. Naturally, the two other fillings that contained mostly air—shaving cream and puffed wheat—were almost as efficient. But the rice, sand, and water provided little pressure and absorbed almost all of the ball's kinetic energy on impact.

Did You Know?

Can you bounce the bounce out of even a good rubber ball? It all depends on how well the rubber retains kinetic energy. The ideal ball surface experiences only elastic deformation—that is, when the ball dents, the rubber molecules stay fixed in place and change only their relative spacing. But even in high-quality commercial rubbers, the molecules slide around and are ripped from their original positions during a dent. This internal molecular friction takes away kinetic energy. Even if most of the molecules return to their original positions, during the next dent more of them will move. Little by little, even a good rubber ball will eventually lose its bounceability.

Plants & Animals

Measure Torque in Vine Growth

Graph the Growth of a Seedling

Compare Seed-Case Swelling in Beans

Migrating Seeds

Seed Observatory

Inhibit Seed Germination

Observe Seedless Germination

Compare Germination in Monocots & Dicots

Starch-Eating Molds

Ethylene: The Ripening Hormone

The Powerful Potato Hormone

Compare Three Plant Tropisms

Symbiosis: Earthworms & Philodendrons

Electrified Earthworm

Extract DNA from Animal Tissue

Do Dogs See in Color?

Measure Torque in Vine Growth

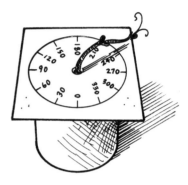

All green plants need light in order to carry out the process of photosynthesis. This is a complex process that allows a plant to manufacture food in the form of carbohydrates from water and oxygen. A light-starved plant will bend toward any source of light in order to survive. When a plant bends toward the light, scientists call this a *phototropic response.*

But plants can demonstrate many different kinds of growth responses. Some plants show rapid and dramatic growth changes in response to outside stimuli. The sunflower, for instance, will twist to follow the motion of the sun each day. Certain vines also behave this way, as you will see in this project.

Sun Motion

Procedure

1. Plant three or four morning-glory seeds in a pot and keep the soil moist. When you see the first sprout, carefully remove that plant and move it to the second pot. Use this plant for your project.

A

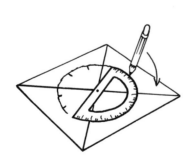

Trace circle and make hatch lines every 30 degrees.

B

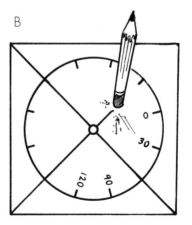

Darken circle and hatch lines. Erase corner lines and mark hatch lines at 30-degree increments.

2. Take a piece of cardboard and trim it into a square that fits nicely over the flowerpot. You should have about 2 inches (5 cm) of space from the tip of each corner of the cardboard to the rim of the pot.

3. Using the ruler and pencil, draw a line on the cardboard connecting each corner to the opposite corner.

4. Punch a hole where the lines meet at the center of the cardboard.

5. Place the center hole of the protractor over the hole you just punched. Trace around the outside edge of the protractor with the pencil and make a hatch line every 30 degrees.

6. Darken the traced circle and hatch lines with the marking pen. Mark each line at 30-degree increments. Erase the pencil lines that connect the corners.

7. If your morning-glory vine is at least 1 inch (2.5 cm) long, carefully poke the tip through the hole in the cardboard and rest the cardboard on top of the flowerpot.

8. Place your project outside or near a large window.

9. Observe and record the movements of the vine regularly each day.

Result

If you keep your morning glory outside, you will find that the vine makes a complete revolution as it traces the path of the sun. If kept near a window, the vine will twist to the window and turn to follow as much sunlight as the window allows.

Tendril Twisting

Procedure

1. When your vine is about 5 inches (12.5 cm) long, remove the cardboard. You may have to enlarge the center hole to avoid damaging the plant.

2. Since graphite is harmful to plants, break the tip off the pencil and push the pencil into the soil, eraser side down, close to the vine.

3. Observe the behavior of the vine for a week and record the result.

Result

As soon as the surface of the vine touches the pencil, the vine responds by growing in a tight coil around the pencil. When it reaches the top of the pencil, the vine will grow straight out again, following the movement of light.

Explanation

The morning glory demonstrates two different growth responses in this project. The first, *phototropism,* is a response to light. When exposed to a light source, the cells on the shaded part of the vine grow more quickly. This causes to the vine to bend toward the source of light. The second, *thigmotropism,* is a response to touch. When one side of the vine touches a surface, the cells of the opposite side grow very quickly. This causes the vine to twine tightly around the pencil. Scientists do not understand this process entirely. But it appears that plant hormones send instructions to the cells to make them grow in response to a stimulus.

Graph the Growth of a Seedling

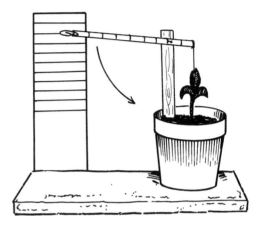

Growth-Measuring Device

You Will Need

- Lima beans or lentils
- 4½-inch (11.25-cm) flowerpot and soil
- 1 × 12-inch balsa-wood strip
- 9-inch (22.5-cm) drinking straw
- Sewing pin
- Thumbtacks
- Thread
- Ruler
- 3 × 14-inch (7.5 × 35-cm) cardboard strip
- 4 × 12-inch (10 × 30-cm) piece of Styrofoam (base)
- Fine-point felt-tip marking pen
- Graph paper
- Paper clip
- Rubber cement

You can measure how quickly a seedling grows to become an adult plant with this simple project. Keep in mind that this project, like any other that requires seed germination, should be begun weeks in advance of your science fair.

Procedure

1. Plant several lima-bean or lentil seeds in small pots. Use the first one that sprouts for your project.

2. Using the ruler and marking pen, divide the drinking straw into 10 equal sections. Push a sewing pin through the mark closest to one end of the straw. Attach a paper clip to the other end of the straw.

3. Push the pin into one end of the balsa-wood strip, attaching the straw to the strip. Make sure the straw pivots against the strip.

4. Push the opposite end of the strip about 2 inches (5 cm) into the soil. The strip should stand right next to the seedling.

5. Carefully make a loop of thread and tighten it around the tip of the seedling. Tie the other end of the thread to the end of the straw. Place a dab of rubber cement over the knot to keep the thread from slipping.

6. Adjust the pivot so that the straw is at a right angle to the pencil. You may have to either push the pencil farther into the soil or adjust the length of the thread.

7. Take the strip of cardboard and, using the ruler and marking pen, divide it into 1-inch (2.5-cm) sections.

8. Attach the cardboard strip to one end of the Styrofoam strip with thumbtacks.

9. Place the plant and pivot on the other end of the Styrofoam strip.

10. Prepare a piece of graph paper so that the vertical edge represents growth in inches or centimeters and the horizontal edge the

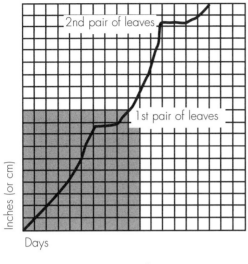

2nd pair of leaves

1st pair of leaves

Inches (or cm)

Days

Bean Seedling
10-Day Maximum Growth Period (in gray)

motion of the straw magnifies the growth of the seedling about 10 times. As you plot the growth pattern of the seedling, you will notice times of great growth activity and times where the growth seems to stop or plateau. During a plateau period, examine the seedling for other signs of growth.

Explanation

Although our graph is designed for a much longer period, the bean seedling shows its most intense period of stem growth in the first 10 days. After the first week, the stem stops growing and tiny leaves begin to sprout. All growth activity is concentrated in the leaves for several days. When the leaves are fully developed, growth in the stem resumes.

Display Tip

Document the assembly of your project with photographs. Display your pivot device alongside the graph you made to contain growth data. The device may be used in a variety of plant-growth experiments, including ones where you determine how differing amounts of light and water can affect plant development.

number of days. Measure the growth of your seedling on this chart.

Result

As your seedling grows, the straw will pivot down along the 1-inch (2.5-cm) markers on the cardboard strip. Since the drinking straw was divided into 10 equal sections, the

Compare Seed-Case Swelling in Beans

You Will Need

- 10 each: lima beans, corn, garbanzos (chick peas), and kidney beans
- 50 dried peas
- Drinking glass
- Paper towel
- 1 cup (240 ml) plaster of paris
- Paper mixing bucket
- Wooden paint stirrer
- Large paper cup
- Plastic washtub

To protect the delicate contents inside, plant seeds often have extremely hard shells. Think of the walnut, for instance, or even the pumpkin seed. But how does the delicate seedling emerge from so tight a container?

Cracking the Bean Case

Procedure

1. Divide each group of lima beans, corn, garbanzo beans, and kidney beans in half.

2. Fill a glass with warm water and drop five of each bean into the glass. Keep the remaining beans dry.

3. Allow the beans to soak overnight. Then empty the water from the glass and place your soaked beans on the paper towel.

4. Compare each group of soaked beans with its dry other half. Record your observations.

Result

The soaked beans have swollen considerably and are softer to the touch. Some may have cracked their seed cases open to reveal the seed embryo inside.

Explanation

Water enters the seed case through cell membranes and is absorbed by the seed embryo. This causes swelling in the embryo, eventually breaking the seed case that contains it. Now the seedling is free to poke through.

The Mighty Pea

Procedure

1. Combine 1 cup (240 ml) of plaster of paris with 2 cups (480 ml) of water in the paint-mixing bucket. Use the stirrer to mix it until the plaster has the consistency of soft putty.

2. Add the 50 dried peas to the plaster and stir them in.

3. Pour the plaster-and-peas mixture into the paper cup.

4. Allow the plaster to dry for about 1 hour. Then carefully peel away the cup, exposing the plaster.

5. Fill the washtub with water and carefully drop the plaster into the water. Check it in several hours, but leave it to soak overnight. Record your observations the next day.

Result

After a few hours, the plaster will begin to show many cracks. By the next morning, it will crack into several pieces, eventually falling apart.

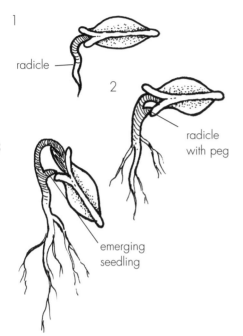

radicle

radicle
with peg

emerging
seedling

Seedling Breaking through Seed Case

Explanation

The pea seeds absorb water through the plaster and begin to swell. The combined force of the swelling seeds breaks the plaster. This is the way many seeds germinate in hard ground or even under asphalt. Never underestimate the strength of a swelling seed!

Did You Know?

Some plants have developed elaborate methods of cracking open their seed cases. For example, the pumpkin seed swells enough to allow the tiny root, called the radicle, to emerge from the tiny opening at the end of the seed case. This opening is called the microphyle. But the microphyle is hardly large enough to allow the stem and developing leaves to emerge. As the stem begins to slide out, it develops a bump on its surface called a peg. This peg acts as a wedge, prying open the microphyle so that it becomes large enough to let the rest of the stem pass through it.

Migrating Seeds

You Will Need

- Thick knee-high cotton socks
- 2 rubber bands
- Shallow bowl
- Water
- Magnifying glass

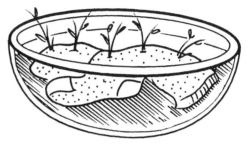

Plants have evolved clever ways of spreading their seeds far and wide. Some flowers, like the fruiting dandelion, have seeds that float on the wind like parachutes and scatter for miles. Certain trees, like the maple and elm, have airplane-shaped seed pods that can fly far from their sources. Animals eat sweet seeds, like the acorn and cherry, and digest the fruit but expel the seed. And coconuts float in the water! But many plants have sticky seeds that simply hitch a ride with anything that passes by—animal, insect, or gym sock.

Procedure

1. Wear high cotton socks and long pants for this project. Pull your socks up over the cuffs of your pants and keep the socks from slipping down with rubber bands.

2. Find a field of tall grass, and slowly walk through it.

CAUTION: Never hike through a field with bare flesh exposed. Many insects can harm you, particularly the deer tick that carries Lyme disease. This pest is found in many parts of the United States and Canada.

3. When you return home, remove your socks and place them in a shallow bowl of room-temperature water. Allow the socks to become completely soaked in the water; then move the bowl with socks to a sunny area.

Result

In about a week, your socks will spring to life as many seeds, caught in the cotton fibers, begin to germinate.

Explanation

Many varieties of grass, such as fescue and cheat, produce seeds with tiny hooks or barbs. This type of seed attaches to fibers or fur. Examine some of the seeds in your socks with a magnifying glass. Although you may find a great variety of seed shapes, all share this hook design.

Display Tip

Your socks, sprouting in a bowl, will certainly attract some attention. Keep a magnifying glass close by. Use a field guide for your area to help you identify some of the grasses. Make a sketch of the more interesting seed shapes, showing some of their common barb structures.

Did You Know?

Seeds are not the only things you or your pet can carry home.

CAUTION: *Urushiol*, the toxic oil of the poison-ivy and poison-oak plants, can stick to clothing and fur and remain dangerous for hours. Always beware of three-leaved plants growing at the base of trees and near water. Wash your clothing immediately, and wear rubber gloves to wash your pet, if you're not sure what sort of plants you've stepped through.

Seed Observatory

What happens when a seed begins its transformation into a plant? Usually this process is hidden from us because most seeds germinate under soil. But you can set up your own small seed observatory to watch a seed come to life.

Note: You may combine this project with the "Inhibit Seed Germination" project.

Procedure

1. If you are using the swollen seeds from the "Inhibit Seed Germination" project, skip to the next step. If you are using new seeds, soak them in water overnight.

2. Stuff the olive jar with as much cotton as possible.

3. Tuck the three seeds between the cotton and the glass, placing them at about the middle of the jar.

4. Add a little water to the jar; then place your hand over the top and tip the jar several times so that the water is absorbed by the cotton. If the cotton is still dry, add more water and repeat this procedure.

5. Place the observatory jar in a warm, light place. Keep the cotton moist by adding water each day.

Seed Observatory

Result

After only a day or two, you will see a tiny root appearing from one side of the seed. Then the seed will crack and you will see a small loop poking out. This will become the stem. Observe the seeds closely. Do root and stem come out of the seed at the same place? You will see that the root comes out of the seed's scarlike opening called the microphyle, while the small loop appears from the seed's crack.

Explanation

A germinating seed will first seek water to nourish the developing shoot. The root will grow toward water—in this case the moist bottom of the paper toweling. The shoot grows upward. The seed itself contains all the nutrients the shoot requires. But as the seed falls away, the shoot must take its nutrients from the environment. This is why you must eventually cover your seedlings in soil for them to develop into healthy plants.

Inhibit Seed Germination

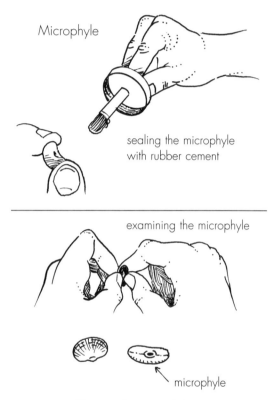

Microphyle

sealing the microphyle
with rubber cement

examining the microphyle

microphyle

<table>
<tr><td>

You Will Need

- 12 lentil or lima beans
- Rubber cement
- Shallow pan
- Water

</td></tr>
</table>

Seeds can remain dormant for years until just the right conditions—water, light, and temperature—allow them to come to life. But how exactly does this happen? What makes an apparently lifeless, dry seed germinate or begin to produce a healthy green shoot? Scientists have even sprouted seeds that were thousands of years old. In this project, you will see how some seeds are designed for germination.

Procedure

1. Examine your 12 seeds, making sure none have cracks or openings in the skin. Examine the seeds carefully. You will notice no marks on them except on one side. There you will see what looks like a scar and a tiny spot at one end of the scar.

2. Take 6 of the seeds and apply a little rubber cement over the scar and tiny spot. Make sure both scar and spot are completely covered. Allow the rubber cement to dry.

3. Fill the shallow pan with water and drop the cemented seeds into the pan. Try to keep the seeds together on one side of the pan.

4. Take the remaining 6 seeds and drop them into the other side of the pan.

5. Allow the seeds to stand overnight.

Result

The cemented seeds look as they did when you put them in the water. The other 6

appear swollen, and some of them may have wrinkled and split their skins.

Explanation

Water enters the bean seed through a little opening near the white scar. The opening was the spot you saw. In six of them you coated the spot with rubber cement so that the water could not get in. This opening is called the microphyle.

Display Tip

Document the assembly of your project with photographs. Make a large drawing of a microphyle and display it next to your pan of water. A germinating seed is fascinating to observe. Place a magnifying glass next to your pan to allow visitors to your project to examine your seeds closely.

Observe Seedless Germination

You Will Need

- Potato, small onion, carrot, philodendron leaves, geranium leaves (*gardening store*)
- Bryophyllum leaf (*gardening store*)
- Rooting hormone-tetramethyl thiuramdisulfide powder (*gardening store*)
- 3 small glasses
- Shallow pan
- Saucer
- 6 small flowerpots
- Potting soil
- Toothpicks
- Sharp knife

This project requires some advance planning since you will have to allow for some growing time. You will see that some plants do not necessarily need seeds to reproduce.

Vegetative Propagation

Procedure

1. Have an adult cut the potato in half and the top from the carrot. With the cut sides down, push a few toothpicks into the half potato and carrot top. Push some toothpicks into the small onion, too.

2. Fill 3 small glasses with water and place 1 tablespoon (15 ml) of rooting hormone in a saucer. Carefully dip the cut sides of the carrot and potato in the rooting hormone. Gently brush the pointed side of the onion in the rooting hormone.

3. Place the potato and carrot each in a glass of water so that the water just touches the cut sides. (You may need to add more water.) Put the onion in a glass so that the pointed end rests underwater. Place all plants in a warm area with lots of light. Make sure you replace the water that evaporates from the glasses each day.

Result

After about a week, you will see small roots appearing from the cut surfaces of the potato and carrot. The pointed end of the onion will have fine, hairlike roots as well. Notice areas on the surface of the potato that begin to change color and shape. Notice the new green growth at the top of the carrot. Notice the straight green shoot that comes from the top of the onion.

Explanation

The potato, onion, and carrot can reproduce through a process called vegetative propagation. The potato is actually an underground stem called a tuber. The small cavities on the outside of the potato, called eyes, are the organs of vegetative reproduction. Each eye can grow into a potato plant that is genetically identical to the parent plant. The onion is another sort of tuber called a bulb. But unlike the potato, the entire onion is the organ of reproduction. The carrot vegetable is also the root of the carrot plant. In this case, the root is the organ of vegetative propagation.

Cell Specialization

Procedure

1. Fill the shallow pan with water and carefully dip the edges of the bryophyllum leaf in the rooting hormone. Place the leaf in the water.

2. Cut several leaves from the philodendron and geranium plants, making sure you have about 1 inch (2.5 cm) of stem on each leaf. Lean each leaf against the side of the pan so that the cut stems are in the water.

3. Place the pan in a warm area with lots of light. Make sure you replace the water that evaporates from the glasses each day.

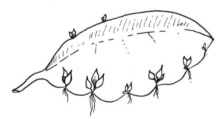

New plants grow at edges of bryophyllum leaf.

Result

The philodendron and geranium leaves will show root development at the cut ends of the stems. But the real surprise is the bryophyllum leaf. Notice how all along the leaf edge, tiny bryophyllum plants have begun to grow. These miniature bryophyllums have both roots and tiny leaves.

Explanation

When the cuttings from certain plants are exposed to the proper conditions, their cells begin to change. Cells that were normally part of the stem begin to turn into root cells. These cells then reproduce very quickly, cre-

ating a root for the cutting. Scientists call this behavior of cells specialization.

Soiling Over

Procedure

1. Fill the 5 small flowerpots with potting soil. Add some water to moisten the soil.

2. Take the bryophyllum leaf, and with an adult's help, carefully cut the smaller plants away from the leaf. Place each small plant on top of the soil in the first pot. Press the soil down around each leaf to form a little well.

3. Take the philodendron leaves and carefully push their stems down into the soil of the second flowerpot.

4. Place the geranium leaves in the third pot.

5. Put the potato in the fourth flowerpot and cover it so that the cut surface is about half under the soil. Do the same for the carrot top.

6. In the last pot, bury the onion so that only the sprouting tip is exposed.

7. Place all plants in a well-lighted area and water each regularly.

Result

With a little care and attention, all of your plants should thrive. The bryophyllums will grow too large for the small pot so that eventually you will have to transplant them. The carrot, too, may be transplanted.

Explanation

If your plants had been left in water, eventually they would die. That's because each growing plant would eventually use up its own nutrients and require minerals from the soil, particularly nitrogen for the roots.

Did You Know?

Scientists have experimented with soil-less growing environments. As a substitute for soil, they have created a nutrient-rich liquid that is sprayed over the exposed roots. This *hydroponic* process would let farmers grow crops vertically without using very much land. It would also allow farming in places that have very poor soil.

Compare Germination in Monocots & Dicots

You Will Need

- Package each: lima-bean, corn, and radish seeds (*OK to substitute lentils for lima beans and mustard seeds for radish seeds*)
- Tall olive jar
- Cotton
- Water

In this project you will see that not all germinating seeds look the same. The difference in germination reflects the two different classes of plants that produce the seeds. In fact, some plants begin without seeds at all. (See "Observe Seedless Germination.")

Note: You may combine this project with the "Seed Observatory" project.

Procedure

1. Take 3 seeds each of lima-bean, corn, and radish and soak them in water overnight.

2. Stuff the olive jar with as much cotton as possible.

3. Tuck the 9 seeds that were soaked in water between the cotton and the glass, placing them at about the middle of the jar. Keep each group of seeds—lima-bean, corn, and radish—together.

4. Add a little water to the jar; then place your hand over the top and tip the jar several times so that the water is absorbed by the cotton. If the cotton is still dry,

add more water and repeat this procedure. Place the jar in a warm, light place. Keep the cotton moist by adding water each day.

Result

After a few days, observe each group of seeds. You will notice a tiny root and small shoot coming out of each seed. But not all of the germinating seeds look alike. You will notice that the germinating lima-bean and radish seeds look alike, except that the radish seed is much smaller. But the corn seed looks different. Where the lima-bean and radish seeds have curved shoots coming out of them, the corn seed has a sharp, straight shoot with a folded top.

Explanation

The lima-bean and radish seeds are called *dicotyledons* because their seeds have two parts. Plants that come from dicotyledon seeds are called dicotyledons, or dicots for short. You can recognize a mature dicot by looking for a branched vein structure in its leaves. The corn seed is called a *monocotyledon* because the seed has only one part. Plants that come from *monocotyledon* seeds are called monocotyledons, or monocots for short. These are the more primitive variety of plants, and you can recognize one by the parallel vein structure in its leaves.

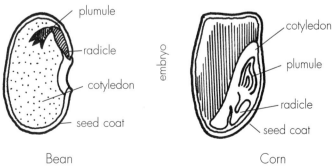

Bean   Corn

Starch-Eating Molds

<table>
<tr><td>

You Will Need

- 3 raw potatoes
- 6 mayonnaise jars with covers
- Pot or saucepan with cover
- Dishwashing gloves
- Soil
- Breadcrumbs
- Hair strand
- Pencil

</td></tr>
</table>

The smallest inhabitants of the plant kingdom—molds—lead very different lives from their green-leaved relatives. Molds don't have roots and flowers, they don't use seeds to reproduce, and they like to clump together in a colony. In fact, the only reason we can see molds is because of this clumping behavior.

Molds are everywhere—in soil, on foods, even in the air we breathe. Some are very dangerous. Others, like the penicillin mold, have been made into powerful medicines. Molds enjoy warm temperatures and moist environments. Some molds feed on sugar and starch and others enjoy fat and protein. When a mold settles on a piece of food it likes, it will quickly reproduce to form a colony.

Closely related to molds are bacteria. These are much smaller than molds, but they like the same foods. Soil contains many different kinds of bacteria. Some are essential for plant growth because they attach to the root and help the plant absorb nitrogen.

This project demonstrates the conditions under which both molds and bacteria thrive. Scientists who study molds and bacteria are called microbiologists. Like a microbiologist, you will cultivate a variety of different molds and bacteria from several sources.

Procedure

1. Wear the dishwashing gloves for this step. Wash the mayonnaise jars and lids in very hot soapy water. Rinse them in hot water and screw on the lids.

2. Boil water in the pot and add the potatoes. Let them cook for about 10 minutes; then turn off the heat. Leave the pot covered while the water cools. When it has cooled to lukewarm, take out the potatoes.

3. Unscrew the lids on the jars. Cut the potatoes in half and place a half-potato with the cut side up in each of the jars. Screw on the lids, but not tightly. Label jar #1 "Clean Potato" and place it aside. This is your control.

4. Poke the tip of the pencil in the soil. Then carefully unscrew the lid of jar #2 and touch the cut surface of the potato in several places with the pencil-lead tip of the pencil. Screw the lid back on, but don't tighten it. Label this jar "Soil."

5. Unscrew the lid of jar #3. Touch your finger to the floor; then gently rub your finger against the cut side of the potato. Screw the lid back on and label this jar "Dirty Finger."

Potatoes in Jars

6. Wash your hands in soapy water. Unscrew the lid of jar #4 and rub your finger across the surface of the potato. Label this jar "Washed finger."

7. Unscrew the lids of jars #5 and 6. Place a strand of your hair on one potato, and sprinkle some breadcrumbs on the other potato. Label the jars.

8. Cover the jars in black construction paper and place them in a sunny area. After a few days, uncover the jars and observe what has happened.

Result

All potato halves show fuzzy patches and small discolored areas. The fuzzy patches are molds and the circular areas are colonies of bacteria. The soiled potatoes appear to have a greater number of colonies than the control potato. But the control potato also shows growth, and these airborne molds and bacteria entered the jar before you were able to screw on the lid. The potatoes you touched with your washed and soiled finger have about the same degree of moldiness. What does this tell you about washing with soap? The potato with the hair and the potato with breadcrumbs show mold and bacteria colonies too, but of a slightly different color. These varieties prefer the protein in hair and gluten protein of the breadcrumbs.

Explanation

Starch-loving molds and bacteria have populated the potato halves. The soiled potato has many more molds that were added from the soil. The clean potato also shows contamination, but from where? Remember, you removed the lids from the jars when you added the potato halves. Molds and bacteria, floating in the air, entered the jars. Although you washed the jars in hot soapy water, only boiling would have sterilized them.

Although all of the molds and bacteria you see liked starch, different varieties of molds and bacteria populated the potatoes according to what contaminant you used. You'll notice different colors on the breadcrumb and hair molds. These molds not only love starch, but sugar (bread) and protein (hair) too.

Note: Both molds and bacteria can be dangerous. After you finish documenting your result, discard your molds carefully. Wash the jars in hot soapy water before recycling them.

Display Tip

Make a chart like the one illustrated to record your observations. Most science fairs do not allow the display of living molds, so it's important that you document your result with photographs.

Ethylene: The Ripening Hormone

You Will Need

- 2 very ripe bananas
- 3 green bananas
- 2 unripe avocados
- 3 brown paper bags
- Stapler
- Felt-tip marking pen

You may have heard the expression "One bad apple spoils the barrel." But you might also say "One ripe banana ripens the rest" or "One red tomato turns the green ones red, too." In this project, you'll demonstrate how a ripening fruit affects the ripening of other fruits.

Procedure

1. Place the first green banana out in the open air, the second green banana in a brown paper bag, and the third green banana in a brown paper bag with the very ripe banana. Staple the bags closed and label them with the felt-tip marking pen.

2. Place the first unripe avocado out in the open and the second avocado in a brown paper bag with the other very ripe banana. Staple the bag closed and label it.

3. Leave the bags undisturbed for 5 days. Then open the bags and compare all the fruits for ripeness.

Result

The green banana and unripe avocado left exposed show signs of slight ripening in the form of softening and brown spots on their skins. The green banana sealed in the bag shows more ripening, but not as much as the green banana sealed in the bag with the very ripe banana. Here you'll find that both bananas have turned nearly black.

As for the avocado sealed in a bag with the second ripe banana—it, too, shows signs of accelerated ripening when compared to the avocado left exposed.

Explanation

Ripening fruit "breathes" in that it takes in oxygen and gives off carbon dioxide. Oxygen stimulates the ripening process. But, mysteriously, ripening fruit also gives off a gas that speeds the ripening of other fruits exposed to the gas. Scientists call this gas *ethylene*, and it's known as the "ripening hormone."

In your project, the fruit placed with the overripe fruit ripened quickly because of the abundance of ethylene gas in the paper bag. There was also some oxygen in this bag, since small amounts of oxygen can pass through paper. As your banana and avocado combination proved, ethylene gas is a common ripening stimulant for various kinds of fruits.

Although less oxygen was present to stimulate the ripening of the banana left in the bag by itself, the fruit eventually began to breathe its own ethylene and ripen more quickly. Fruits left exposed to the air had plenty of oxygen to help them ripen, but their ripening hormone was lost to air currents and carried away.

Did You Know?

Commercial food manufacturers sometimes use ethylene to force greenhouse fruit to ripen, as is the case with the "gassed" tomatoes you buy in the winter. Gassing, however, does not allow a fruit or vegetable starch to turn into sugar as thoroughly, and so a gassed tomato will never taste as flavorful as a naturally ripened one.

In case you're wondering, a tomato is a fruit and not a vegetable. Here's a good rule for telling the difference: If the seeds are on the inside, it's a fruit; if the seeds are on the outside, it's a vegetable.

The Powerful Potato Hormone

You Will Need

- 2 small potatoes
- Plastic gardening flat
  (*gardening store*)
- Knife
- Potting soil

All sorts of mysterious chemical reactions occur inside a germinating plant. For example, how do plants know to grow in the direction of sunlight and water? How do they learn that their roots should grow down and their stems up?

Scientists believe the answer to this question has to do with growth hormones produced in a developing plant. These hormones can instruct the plant's stem cells to grow faster on one side than on the other, causing the plant to bend in the direction of light. The same hormones will tell root cells to divide quickly so that the root will seek water. As you'll see in this project, hormones can even instruct a plant not to grow.

Potatoes also have hormones. The potato, which is actually a large underground stem called a *tuber*, does not have seeds but reproduces through the spuds (the eyes) on its skin. The spud is the reproductive organ of the potato. To raise potatoes, farmers cut them to pieces and bury them in mineral-rich soil.

Procedure

1. Fill the gardening flat with potting soil and place it in a warm, well-lighted place.

2. Take one of the potatoes and examine its surface for spuds. These are the small cavities where a new potato plant will grow.

3. With an adult's help, cut this potato into many pieces. Make sure that there is at least one spud on each piece.

4. Bury each potato piece in the gardening flat.

5. Bury the second potato whole in the gardening flat.

6. Water the flat regularly.

7. Wait 3 weeks and then "unbury" all potatoes to examine them.

Result

After 3 weeks, all of your potatoes should produce healthy plants. But whereas the whole potato has only one plant growing from a spud, each potato piece has a plant growing from its spud. This means that the whole potato used only one of its spuds to produce an offspring.

Explanation

Scientists believe that when planted, the whole potato produces a hormone that travels throughout the body of the potato. This hormone allows only one spud to germinate and switches all the other spuds off so that they remain dormant. Because of this, the new growth will not have to share its supply of water and minerals with competing plants. The pieces of cut potato should each produce a healthy plant since each piece contains only one spud. However, if you find a piece with two spuds, only one of them will be sprouting. Again, the powerful potato hormone has switched off the competing growth.

Compare Three Plant Tropisms

Note: Use the potato plant in the "Observe Seedless Germination" project.

To find the water, light, and minerals they need to survive, plants mysteriously know in which direction to grow. This type of growth is called a *tropism*. The following project demonstrates the three basic kinds of plant tropisms: *hydrotropism*, growth toward water; *geotropism*, growth toward the pull of gravity; and *phototropism*, growth toward light.

Hydrotropism

Procedure

1. With an adult's help, cut the gallon (or 4-L) milk container in half and save the bottom portion. Cut out a square from the flat bottom.

2. Use the wire cutters to cut a piece of screen that will fit over the square. Place the screen over the square and fasten it with a little tape.

3. Moisten a little potting soil with water so that it clumps together. Gently spoon soil into the milk container, covering the screen. If the soil spills through the screen, add more water to it.

4. Place the lima-bean seeds in the center of the soil, over the screen. Cover the seeds with more soil, and put the milk container over the saucer.

5. Use the spray bottle to keep the soil moist, not wet. Avoid having excess water drip through the screen and into the saucer. If that happens, replace the wet saucer with a dry one.

Result

After about 10 days, lift the milk container from the saucer and look at the screen underneath. You should see small roots poking straight down, then abruptly looping back toward the screen.

Hydrotropism

Explanation

The downward growth of the lima-bean roots is in response to the Earth's gravity (geotropism). But soon the roots discover that the water they need is in the soil above them. Cells on one side of the root grow faster than cells on the other side, so the root turns and starts to grow up toward the soil. You can see that finding water is more important to a lima-bean seed than following the law of gravity.

Geotropism

Procedure

1. Remove the glass panes from two photo frames. Cut a piece of blotting paper or felt the same dimensions of the glass, and place it on one of the panes. Sprinkle a few radish seeds in the center of the felt, and cover the felt with the second pane of glass, like a sandwich.

2. Loop two rubber bands horizontally at the top and bottom edges of the sandwich, and two more rubber bands vertically at the left and right edges.

3. Place the sandwich on its edge in the shallow pie plate. Keep it standing upright by pressing two lumps of modeling clay around each corner.

4. With the eyedropper, add enough water to the sandwich's top edge so that water seeps between the two panes of glass, wetting the radish seeds.

5. Continue to water, and in about a week you'll see root hairs against the felt, growing straight down.

6. When the hairs become long enough, rotate the sandwich on its next edge, secure it with clay, and continue watering for another week.

7. Continue rotating the sandwich, waiting a week between each turn, until the sandwich is in its original position.

Result

In response to the rotation, the roots will abruptly change direction so that they always grow down. With enough water and patience, your roots will trace a delicate spiral pattern.

Phototropism

Procedure

1. Remove the cover of the shoebox and place it aside. With an adult's help, carefully cut a 2-inch (5-cm) hole in one end of the shoebox.

2. Cut the cardboard into 3 strips as wide as the shoebox is deep and about three-fourths the width of the shoebox. Make a narrow fold along the strips at one end, and tape them inside the box at equal distances apart, alternating sides. You should have three baffles and a small chamber at the rear of the shoebox.

Geotropism

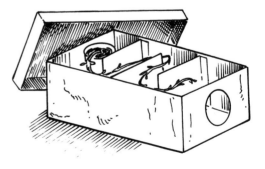

Phototropism

3. Place the potato plant in the small chamber and put the lid on the shoebox. Position the shoebox in a window with the hole facing the light. Open the box only to water the potato periodically and to observe plant growth.

Result

The shoots from the potato plant will snake around the baffles toward the light at the end of the box.

Display Tip

Display your three plant-tropism samples side by side with an explanation of each. Remember, you need to plan well ahead for this project—your plants need to be fairly well developed to demonstrate these principles.

Symbiosis: Earthworms & Philodendrons

How beneficial are earthworms to plant life? What can the lowly *annelid* do to bring a rose to its fullest glory or help a tomato seed sprout into a fruiting plant? With a couple of philodendrons and a few healthy worms, you can find out.

Start your earthworm-gathering early. You should also allow ample time for the plants to develop so that you can watch for a significant result. The best time to find earthworms is after a rainstorm or during wet mornings. The worms come to the surface to enjoy the moisture and can be easily found along the sides of sidewalks or driveways. If you don't find any worms on the surface, remove a 2-inch (5-cm) layer of moist soil from the garden, then shake out the soil from your trowel. You should find several earthworms in the soil.

Procedure

1. Remove the labels from the bottles and cut off the tops so that you have 2 clear plastic cylinders. Use the sharp nail to punch 3 holes in the bottom of each bottle, and place each bottle on a plate.

2. Place a layer of soil in the first cylinder; then add a layer of cornstarch. Continue adding layers of soil and cornstarch until the cylinder is about two-thirds full; then insert a philodendron plant and add enough soil to cover the roots. Press the soil down tightly, compressing it around the plant. Label this cylinder "A."

3. Repeat step #2 for the second cylinder, but add four or five earthworms as a last step. Label this cylinder "B."

4. Cover the cylinders with black construction paper, and keep the plants in a warm, well-lighted place, watering them regularly.

5. After a few weeks, compare the plants. Which philodendron appears healthier? Remove the construction paper from the cylinders and compare the soils.

Result

The philodendron in cylinder B containing the earthworms appears larger and healthier. The soil and cornstarch in this cylinder have been mixed together so that you can hardly recognize the layers. In cylinder A, the layers remain intact.

Explanation

Adding earthworms to cylinder A helped the philodendron. Earthworms benefit plants in many ways, and in turn, a healthy plant returns the favor. This kind of mutually advantageous relationship between two living organisms is called *symbiosis*.

As earthworms tunnel, they ingest the soil, feeding on any organic matter they find. (You can see evidence of earthworm tunneling in the destruction of the cornstarch layers.) This matter is excreted in earthworm *casting*, which fertilizes the soil and contains important minerals such as nitrogen, phosphorous, potassium, as well as other micronutrients important to plants. Plants in turn provide much of the decaying organic matter on which earthworms love to feast. Worms also add calcium carbonate, a compound that helps moderate soil pH. This can change a more acidic or alkaline soil to neutral.

Although they are the most numerous in the top 6 inches (15 cm), earthworms also work in the subsoil, bringing mineral-rich soil from below to the surface. This adds to the supply of nutrients available to plants. Scientists know that in 100 square feet (9 square meters) of soil, earthworms may bring from 4 to 6 pounds (1.8 to 2.7 kg) of subsoil dirt to the soil surface each year.

Worms also spread their casting, mixing it thoroughly within the top 12 inches (30 cm) of soil. They may also mix it as far down as 6 feet (1.8 m). And a soil that's rich in humus may easily support 25 worms per cubic foot (0.03 cubic meter), which translates into at least 175 pounds (about 78 to 80 kg) of fertilizer per year for a 200-square-foot (18-square-meter) garden. This means that your garden or lawn can be supplied with far more fertilizer, and of superior quality, than 10 to 20 pounds (4.5 to 9 kg) of a commercial fertilizer. So earthworms save us money, too!

Finally, earthworm tunnels help to aerate and loosen the soil. This allows more oxygen and water in, which not only stimulates root growth, but also improves conditions for certain beneficial soil bacteria. The tunneling also provides access to deeper soil levels for the numerous smaller organisms that contribute to the health of the soil.

Did You Know?
Earthworms are prodigious multipliers, reproducing even faster than rabbits. Ten pounds (4.5 kg) of earthworms can become over 2 tons (1.8 metric tons) in 2 years!

Electrified Earthworm

This project shows how some animals use electromagnetic fields to help them find their way around. Look for worms at the edges of pavement after a rainy day, or use a trowel to dig about 2 or 3 inches (5 or 7.5 cm) down into moist soil until you find a worm. The current from the battery will not harm the worm.

Procedure

1. Use the scissors to strip about a ½ inch (1.25 cm) of plastic coating from each end of the insulated wires.

2. Turn the D-cell on its side. Tape one end of one wire to the positive terminal and one end of the other wire to the negative terminal.

3. Fold two sheets of newspaper into a 4 × 6-inch square (10 × 15-cm square)— the size will depend on the size of your worm.

4. Pour water over the newspaper pad, soaking it thoroughly.

Electrified Worm Set-up

5. Put the worm on the center of the pad. It will probably wriggle quite a bit at first but soon calm down.

6. Touch the positive wire to the newspaper about 1 inch (2.5 cm) from one end of the worm. Touch the negative wire to the same distance from the opposite end of the worm. Record your result.

Result

The worm either stretches out or contracts into an accordion shape. If the positive terminal is at the worm's head and the negative terminal at its tail, the worm will contract. If the terminals are reversed, the worm will stretch out. Since it can be difficult to tell the head and tail of a worm apart, this is one way to find out!

Explanation

A weak electrical current travels through the worm's body. This current gives the worm information about the conditions of its environment. Although no one knows the exact reasons for this, a current moving in one direction through a worm seems to indicate danger, while a current moving in the opposite direction tells the worm it's safe to stretch out and continue its burrowing.

Did You Know?

"Follow Your Nose": Scientists believe that certain cells in the bodies of animals contain the mineral magnetite (an oxide of iron) and so are magnetic. These "magnetic cells" could help certain animals find food or migrate.

Honeybees, pigeons, tuna, dolphins, and whales all have cells containing magnetite in certain parts of their brains. Scientists now believe that the dolphin, for instance, uses the pull of the North Pole to tell up from down—important information for the dolphin when if must come to the surface to breathe. And whales often become stranded in areas where the magnetic field of the Earth shows some irregularity.

Even humans have small amounts of magnetite in their bodies. Although the amounts are extremely small and difficult to detect, magnetic cells exist in the lining of our noses. Some scientists now believe that at one time our noses were like compasses!

Extract DNA from Animal Tissue

You Will Need

- ½ cup (120 ml) raw chicken livers
- Dishwashing liquid detergent
- Meat tenderizer
- Rubbing alcohol
- Blender
- Strainer
- Glass measuring cup
- Drinking glass
- Small screw-top jar
- Teaspoon or 5-ml spoon
- Paper clip
- Microscope slide and microscope (optional)

All living things contain an amazing blueprint of life in the form of deoxyribonucleic acid, or DNA. The individual genes of the DNA molecule determine much about a plant or animal, including its susceptibility to certain diseases. You can extract DNA easily from several types of plant and animal tissue. This project uses raw chicken livers for a particularly abundant DNA load.

Procedure

1. Put ½ cup (120 ml) of raw chicken livers into a blender and add about ¼ cup (60 ml) of water. Blend the chicken livers until soupy.

CAUTION: Raw chicken and chicken livers can be comtaminated with salmonella bacteria. Wash your hands and everything that the chicken touches in hot soapy water. Cooking well usually kills salmonella.

2. Pour the blended chicken-liver solution through a strainer back into the measuring cup.

3. Observe how much chicken-liver solution you have, and add about one-third more to it of liquid detergent. Gently stir the solution with a teaspoon.

4. Add 1 teaspoon (5 ml) of meat tenderizer to the solution and stir carefully for about 7 minutes. Be patient and don't stir too rapidly or you might break up the delicate strands of DNA in the solution.

5. Carefully pour a portion of the stirred solution into the drinking glass.

6. Tilt the glass and slowly pour rubbing alcohol against the side of the glass until you have about as much alcohol as liver solution. Wait 30 seconds and observe the solution. After about 10 minutes, a quantity of stringy material should begin to appear in the liver solution. This is the isolated DNA.

7. Fill a small jar with alcohol.

8. Straighten the paper clip and bend one end into a small hook. Dip the hook into the solution where the water and alcohol meet, and gently drag some of the water containing the DNA into the alcohol layer.

Wait a few more minutes. Then remove a sample of DNA as it floats to the top of the alcohol. Place a sample on a microscope slide and observe it through the microscope.

9. Repeat step #8, placing the DNA you extracted directly into the alcohol jar to preserve it.

10. Empty the glass and wash it. Then repeat step #6 until you've used all the solution.

Result

Under a microscope, the spiral form of the DNA is evident.

Explanation

Blending the chicken livers broke up the cell walls and cell organs so that the DNA floats around in a soup of protein and fat molecules. Detergent, by its emulsifying action, attracts the fats and pulls it away from the proteins. But the strands of DNA are still protected by a protein coating. To break through this coating and expose the pure DNA, you added the meat tenderizer. The final rendering of DNA requires the alcohol. When added to the solution, the alcohol formed a layer. The lighter strands of DNA floated to the surface of this layer, while the heavier remains of proteins and fats are still in the solution.

Do Dogs See in Color?

You Will Need

- Puppy under 1 year old
- Camera with monochromatic film
- 6 sheets of stationery paper in graduated shades of gray (*office-supply store*)
- 24 sheets of colored stationery, divided into 4 sets (yellows, blues, reds, greens) with 6 sheets each in graduated shades of yellow, blue, red, and green (6 different yellows, 6 different blues, etc.)
- Duplicate set of colored papers, as above
- Felt-tip marking pen (*for numbering*)
- Dog treats
- Friend to assist
- Notebook (*for recording test result*)
- Lots of patience

Whether or not dogs can perceive color has been debated among scientists for many years. Today, sophisticated instruments allow scientists to study the dog's eye and vision with a degree of accuracy unimagined 25 years ago. The debate isn't over, but this project will help you decide which side of the controversy you'll join.

For this project to work, you must minimize variables and choose a training area with few distractions. Do *not* mix types or sizes of papers, and keep your papers in a closed box between training sessions. You must also give yourself ample time for a sufficient training period—at least 9 weeks.

Procedure

1. Place 6 numbered shades of yellow paper against 6 numbered shades of gray paper and shoot a black-and-white photograph. Repeat this for the 6 shades of blue, red, and green paper.

2. When you develop the photos, pair up each shade of color with its closest equivalent shade of gray. Use clean (unnumbered) sheets for the experiment.

3. Choose a well-lighted, quiet place to carry out your experiment. On the ground, place a sheet of yellow paper next to a sheet of gray paper. Separate the papers widely enough so that you can clearly see your dog choose one piece of paper over the other.

4. Stand a few feet behind the papers and have a friend hold the dog about 6 feet (1.8 m) from the papers, facing you.

5. Call the dog. When the dog approaches the papers, he'll sniff to examine them. At that point give the command "Color!" and gently hold the dog's head over the yellow paper. Reward the dog with a treat.

6. Repeat this training every day for about 3 weeks. Then, whether you see a result or not, switch the yellow paper for the blue paper and continue training for another 2 weeks. Follow this with 2 weeks of red paper and 2 weeks of green paper. Remember, each colored paper must be paired with its equivalent shade of gray paper.

7. Carefully record the behavior of your dog throughout each color-training session. Count up the number of times your dog "chooses" each colored paper over the gray paper and compare this to the total number of tests for each training session.

Result

Without drawing firm conclusions, we can say that your dog will make significantly more "correct" (color) choices than incorrect choices, and that this number will vary according to the color of paper used for each session.

The Latest on Dog Vision: The general consensus among scientists today is that dogs may have some form of color vision, but that color isn't particularly valuable information to them and so they tend to ignore it. Although herbivores might have the ability to see color in order to recognize ripe fruits and edible plants, for a terrestrial carnivore like the dog, it's probably more important to detect the shape of objects and to track motion—particularly in dim light. This is supported by the fact that dogs have many more *rods* at the central portion of their retinas than do humans. Rods are the cells that are sensitive to low light and not particularly sensitive to color.

But the question remains—do dogs really see color? After all, the result of your project seemed to indicate that *something* was going on. The latest research supports the theory that dogs do indeed have color vision, but that it's *dichromatic.*

This means that dogs see only part of the range of colors in the spectrum and not the entire spectrum of colors that we humans—with our *trichromatic* color vision—see. Dogs probably lack the ability to see the range of colors from green to red. This means that they see mostly in shades of yellow and blue.

Stars & Planets

Big Dipper: An Alien's Point of View

Simulate the Dust Storms of Mars

Soil Sampling for Microorganisms

Calculate the Relative Distances of Planets

Calculate the Relative Sizes of Planets

Measure Atmospheric Reflection, or "Earth Shine"

Demonstrate the Pulse of Pulsars

Construct a Classic Gnomon Sundial

Use Solar Radiation to Distill Water

Planetary Surface Illusions

Calculate Time from Stellar Motion

Construct a Daytime Moon Locator

Simulate a Partial & Full Solar Eclipse

Compare Standard & Mean Astronomical Time

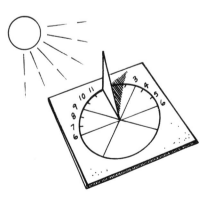

Big Dipper: An Alien's Point of View

The shapes of the constellations, as we know them, would vanish for an observer in another solar system. Stars exist everywhere in the vastness of space and at greatly varying distances from Earth. This means that what we recognize as a constellation is actually a stellar configuration that spans thousands of light-years and would look very different from another vantage point in space. In this project you'll recreate the Big Dipper in the constellation Ursa Major and then view it as a distant observer might.

The Grid of Light-Years

Procedure

1. Use the yardstick and yellow pencil to divide the poster board into a grid of 140 1½-inch (3.75-cm) squares. With the poster board in the horizontal position, make 10 hatch marks 1½ inches (3.75 cm) apart on the left and right edges. Then make 14 hatch marks 1½ inches (3.75 cm) apart at the top and bottom edges. Connect top and bottom hatch marks with lines and connect left and right hatch marks with lines.

2. With the yellow pencil, write "1" in the bottom left-hand corner box. Continue numbering the boxes above it until you reach 10.

3. Starting from the "1" box, use the red pencil to number the boxes to the right until you reach 14. The red numbers represent the X coordinate (horizontal) and the yellow numbers represent the Y coordinate (vertical). Each successive row represents light-years from Earth, with the first row repre-

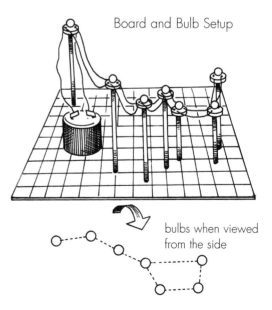

Board and Bulb Setup

bulbs when viewed from the side

senting 50 light-years, and each row above representing an additional 25 light-years.

4. Spread some white glue on the Styrofoam and press the poster board over it. Allow the glue to dry.

5. Cut 3 wooden dowels down to 11¼ inches (28 cm). Cut one dowel to 9½ inches (about 24 cm). Cut the remaining dowels to 9 inches (about 22 cm), 6¾ inches (about 17 cm), and 6 inches (15 cm).

6. Sharpen one end of each dowel with the pencil sharpener.

7. Use the glue gun to attach the bulb holders to the flat end of each dowel. Screw the flashlight bulbs into the bulb holders.

8. Cut the blue wire into 7 pieces with these lengths: 12 inches (30 cm), 10 inches (25 cm), 7 inches (17.5 cm), 5 inches (12.5 cm), 4 inches (10 cm), 3 inches (7.5 cm), and 2 inches (5 cm).

STAR	COORDINATES
Alkaid (11¼" dowel)	X1, Y9
Mizar (11¼" dowel)	X5, Y3
Alioth (9½" dowel)	X6, Y2
Megrez (9" dowel)	X8, Y3
Phekda (6" dowel)	X9, Y3 (shift slightly to right)
Merak (6¾" dowel)	X12, Y3
Dubhe (11¼" dowel)	X13, Y4 (shift slightly to left)

9. Cut the yellow wire into 7 pieces of the same length.

10. Wrap blue construction paper around the 6-volt battery and tape it.

Assembling the Big Dipper

Procedure

1. Seven stars make up the Big Dipper, and each of your dowel-and-bulb pieces represents a star. You must assemble the Dipper star by star by pushing the sharp end of each star into the Styrofoam on an X–Y coordinate of the grid. The chart below lists the stars of the Dipper and where you should put them. Each set of coordinates represents the exact center of a box unless otherwise indicated.

2. Connect the 10-inch (25-cm) piece of blue wire from one terminal of the battery to one terminal of the first star (Alkaid). Connect the 12-inch (30-cm) piece to the corresponding terminal of Mizar, and continue connecting the stars until you've used all the blue wire.

3. Repeat this procedure with the yellow wire so that all bulbs are connected in a parallel circuit and light up (see diagram).

4. Dim the lights and view the stars by standing directly in front of them. You may have to adjust the heights of the dowels slightly.

Result

If you've positioned yourself correctly, you will see the shape of the Big Dipper emerge from the configuration of your stars. Remember, this is only an apparent shape and represents a vantage point from the Earth. As you move around the constellation, the shape of the Dipper will change and quickly become unrecognizable. Moving left, you'll see a configuration that would be visible from the vantage point of the star Arcturus in the constellation Bootes. Moving right presents a view from the star Denebola at the farthest point of Ursa Major, The Bear.

Simulate the Dust Storms of Mars

You Will Need

- Shallow cardboard box
- Plaster of paris
- Brown tempera paint
- Cardboard mixing bucket
- Old tablespoon or 15-ml spoon
- Granulated sugar
- Finely ground coffee
- 5 index cards
- Felt-tip marking pen
- Camera with flash

For years, observers of Mars were puzzled by the changing surface features of the Red Planet. Besides the dramatic shrinking and swelling of the polar caps, large regions of Mars seemed to darken and lighten, and many serious astronomers thought that this was due to seasonal changes in vegetation patterns. But the *Viking* landing eventually revealed the truth. Huge dust storms reveal new surface features while hiding old ones. This means that whole regions of the planet can change color and texture as winds—traveling upwards of 300 miles per hour (480 km per hour)—scour the dry, unstable surface. With the aid of a camera, this project demonstrates how blowing debris can dramatically alter the observable features of Mars.

Martian Terrain

Procedure

1. Mix enough plaster and water in the bucket to make a thick putty. Add some brown tempera paint until the putty turns a coffee color.

2. Spill the putty into the cardboard box and, working quickly, spread the putty around with the back of the tablespoon so that you create a "terrain" of shallow valleys and ridges. Allow this terrain to dry.

3. Sprinkle just enough granulated sugar on the terrain to nearly cover it. Place the index card with the letter "A" written on it in the corner of the box.

4. Hold the camera over the box so that you can frame a full photograph of the terrain. Avoid having the floor or tabletop appear in your photo.

5. Photograph this Martian terrain in its "base state."

6. Move to one side of the box and blow across the terrain so that the granulated sugar moves and accumulates in different places. Place the letter "B" index card in the corner of the box.

7. Holding the camera in the same position as before, photograph the altered terrain.

8. Move to the opposite side of the box and blow again. Place the letter "C" index card in the box and take another photograph.

9. Carefully tip the box over a wastebasket so that the granulated sugar spills out. Replace the granulated sugar with finely ground coffee.

10. Blow the coffee across the terrain in two directions as before, labeling each box "D" and "E" before taking photographs.

Result

Your photos will show conspicuous changes in the Martian terrain from the four storms you created. Use photograph A, which displays the base-state terrain, as the first in your sequence. Follow this photo with photos B through E. The differences among the photos will be dramatic.

Soil Sampling for Microorganisms

You Will Need

- 3 small glass jars
- Bowl
- Large pot
- Tongs
- Towel
- Commercial sand (*aquarium store*)
- Salt
- Sugar
- Baking powder
- 2 yeast cubes
- Measuring spoon
- Measuring cups
- Long ice-tea or ice-cream-soda spoon
- Wide masking tape
- Felt-tip marking pen

This project simulates some of the soil-testing techniques that were used by the *Viking* explorer when it was sent to Mars in 1976. Soil samples were taken aboard the spacecraft, flooded with nutrient-rich solutions, stimulated with light, and exposed to warm temperatures. All of these conditions maximized the environmental conditions optimal for the growth and reproduction of microorganisms. The detection of life was carried out by monitoring the samples for gas emissions, temperature changes, weight irregularities, and prolonged—rather than reactionary—chemical activity.

Procedure

1. Place the three jars in the large pot and fill the pot with enough water to entirely cover the jars. Remove the jars and heat the water to boiling.

2. Using the tongs, carefully drop the jars into the boiling water. Keep them there for about 30 seconds before removing them with the tongs and placing them on the towel to dry.

3. When the jars have cooled, fill each jar with sand to about one-third of its volume.

4. Using the long teaspoon, mix 2 teaspoons (10 ml) of salt into the sand of jar 1 and label it "SALT" with the masking tape and felt-tip marking pen.

5. Mix 2 teaspoons (10 ml) of baking powder into the sand of jar 2 and label it.

6. Crush up the yeast cubes and add them to the sand of jar 3. Label it.

7. To simulate the cold temperatures of Mars, place the 3 jars in the refrigerator and allow them to stay there overnight.

8. The next day, mix ½ cup (120 ml) of sugar into 4 cups (960 ml or about 1 L) of warm water. Use the bowl for this.

9. Remove the jars from the refrigerator and add equal amounts of sugar water to each jar.

10. Place the jars in a well-lighted place and watch them for about 10 minutes. Then leave them undisturbed for an hour.

Result

After an hour, each jar has reacted differently to the sugar water. The salt jar shows no apparent reaction at all and looks just as it did an hour ago. The baking-soda jar became foamy and cloudy when you first added the sugar water, but that reaction is long over and the foam is flat. But the yeast jar continues to react to the sugar water by foaming continually and roiling the sand at the jar's bottom.

Explanation

When testing for life, scientists must carefully distinguish between inert and organic chemical reactions. There are many substances found in soil (like calcium) or conditions of the soil, like its acidic or basic (acid or base) nature, that might react to the chemicals of a nutrient solution. However, these reactions are quick, immediate, and do not suggest the complex organic chemical reactions of microorganisms. In contrast, the jar containing the yeast indicates just such a reaction as the yeast consumes the sugar and multiplies. To everyone's disappointment, the life-seeking experiments of *Viking* did not yield such a dramatic result.

Calculate the Relative Distances of Planets

You Will Need

- Large regional street map (such as New York City map)
- Calculator
- Sewing pins
- Tape measure
- Modeling clay
- Small notepad
- Felt-tip marking pen

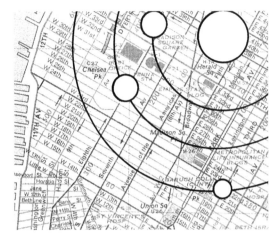

It's impossible to imagine the staggering distances of space. Even our own solar system, so neatly represented in drawings and models, is in reality an enormous system of orbiting planets and moons. To give some idea of the great distances separating even our closest planetary neighbors, scientists create scale reductions. This involves translating planetary distances down to their proportional equivalents so that an entire astronomical system can be reconstructed and more easily understood.

In this project you'll use maps and sewing pins to show the relative distances between all the planets of the solar system. In doing this, you will translate astronomical distances into geographical distances. To begin, examine the chart to understand the relative distances of planets from the Sun. Then you'll translate this information into much smaller proportional equivalents.

When studying the chart, it's important to realize that planets do not orbit around the Sun in perfect circles but in ovoid ellipses. This means that planet-to-Sun distances will vary according to where a planet is along the course of its ellipse. To simplify calculations, the distances recorded in the chart represent the *average* distance of a planet from the Sun.

Calculating Superior & Inferior Planetary Distances

To calculate the relative distances of the planets within our solar system, you must

Distance from Sun	Mercury	Venus	Earth	Mars	Jupiter	Saturn	Uranus	Neptune	Pluto
Miles in millions	36	67.2	93	141.6	483.6	886.7	1,783	2,794	3,666
Km in millions	57.9	108.2	149.6	227.9	778	1,426	2,871	4,497	5,913

first distinguish the *superior planets*, that is, planets that lie outside the Earth's orbit, from the *inferior planets*, those that lie inside the Earth's orbit. From the chart you can see that Mars, Jupiter, Saturn, Uranus, Neptune, and Pluto are superior planets while Venus and Mercury are inferior planets. Using the Earth-to-Sun distance as a base and starting with Pluto, divide the distance of each superior planet with the Earth-to-Sun distance. This gives you the following data:

Pluto Distance (from Sun) ÷ Earth-to-Sun
Distance = 40
Pluto is 40 times more distant from the
Sun than Earth.

To calculate distance for the inferior planets, divide the Earth-to-Sun distance first by the distance of Mercury and then by the distance of Venus. Convert the decimals to fractions.

Earth-to-Sun Distance ÷ Mercury Distance
from Sun = 2.5
Mercury is four-tenths ($^4/_{10}$) the distance of the
Earth to the Sun.

Scaling Planetary Distances to a Regional Map

Now that you have basic relational distances, it's time to scale those distances so that you can place them over a large regional map. Reducing to scale must take into account two factors: the relative distances of planets from the Sun and the relative sizes of planets to each other and to the Sun. Calculating the relative sizes of all the planets is something we save for another project. But for now, think of Earth as an orange and our solar system the greater metropolitan area of New York City, which we'll use for our example. You can, of course, substitute any comparable metropolitan area (with its associated districts, streets, and landmarks) for your solar system.

Again, as a base measurement, use the Earth-to-Sun distance. Remember that the distance of the farthest planet, Pluto, is 40 times greater than the Earth-to-Sun distance, so plot your first distance carefully.

Let's say that the Sun sits in the lobby of the Empire State Building on 34th Street and the Earth sits in the middle of Grand Central Station at 42nd Street. Using the ruler, measure the distance between the Empire State Building and Grand Central Station. This represents the Sun-to-Earth distance of 93 million miles (148.8 million km) and will be the base from which you calculate all other planetary distances. Position the needle of the compass on the Empire State Building and the pencil on Grand Central Station on your map. Sweep the pencil end of the compass around so that you draw a circle representing the orbit of the Earth around the Sun. Place a sewing pin on each location.

Using the relational distances you calculated earlier, determine the positions of the inferior planets Mercury and Venus and draw their orbits using the compass. You can place a sewing pin anywhere along the path of these orbits to indicate the relative position of each planet to the Sun. But for the sake of clarity, let's place our planets in a northerly direction so that, from the Sun at 34th Street, Mercury would be at 37th Street and Venus would be at 40th Street.

Now, using the same calculations, determine the positions of the superior planets and draw their orbits. Continuing north from the Sun at 34th Street, place Mars at 47th Street at Midtown, Jupiter at 105th Street near the top of Central Park, and Saturn at 134th Street in Harlem. The planet Uranus would be at 244th Street in Riverdale, Neptune on the north side of the city of Yonkers, and Pluto way up in Tarrytown, New York, 22 miles from the Empire State Building.

Use the compass to draw the orbit of each inferior and superior planet and indicate their positions with sewing pins. Use the notepad and marker to label each planet on the map. You can also attach a small lump of clay to the head of each pin to approximate the sizes of the various planets.

Relative Distances of Planets to the Sun

Pluto Distance (from Sun) ÷ Earth-to-Sun Distance = 40
Pluto is 40x more distant from the Sun than Earth.

Neptune Distance ÷ Earth-to-Sun Distance = 30
Neptune is 30x more distant from the Sun than Earth.

Uranus Distance ÷ Earth-to-Sun Distance = 19
Uranus is 19x more distant from the Sun than Earth.

Saturn Distance ÷ Earth-to-Sun Distance = 9.5
Saturn is 9.5x more distant from the Sun than Earth.

Jupiter Distance ÷ Earth-to-Sun Distance = 2.25
Jupiter is 2.25x more distant from the Sun than Earth.

Mars Distance ÷ Earth-to-Sun Distance = 1.5
Mars is 1.5x more distant from the Sun than Earth.

Earth-to-Sun Distance ÷ Venus Distance = 1.4
Venus is seven-tenths ($^7/_{10}$) the distance of the Earth to the Sun.

Earth-to-Sun Distance ÷ Mercury Distance (from Sun) = 2.5
Mercury is four-tenths ($^4/_{10}$) the distance of the Earth to the Sun.

Calculate the Relative Sizes of Planets

You Will Need

- Large piece of mural paper
- Felt-tip marking pen
- Compass
- Tape measure
- String
- Pencil
- Transparent tape

The planets of the solar system vary greatly in size. To give us some idea of just how enormous these differences are, scientists create scale reductions. This means that they reduce planetary diameters to their proportional equivalents so that it's easier to compare the sizes of planets to each other and to the Sun. In this project you will create a scaled drawing representing all the planets in our solar system.

To begin, examine the chart on page 187, which lists planetary diameters in miles. Using the calculator, you'll translate this information into much smaller proportional equivalents.

Identifying Superior & Inferior Planets

To calculate the relative sizes of the planets within our solar system, you must first distinguish the *superior planets*, that is, the planets that lie outside of the Earth's orbit, from the *inferior planets*, those that lie inside the Earth's orbit. From the chart you can see that Mars, Jupiter, Saturn, Uranus, Neptune, and Pluto are superior planets while Venus and Mercury are inferior planets.

Calculating Superior Planet Sizes

Begin by using your calculator to divide the diameter of the largest superior planet, Jupiter, by the diameter of the smallest superior planet, Pluto. Continue using Pluto to divide Saturn, Uranus, Neptune, Mars, and Earth. You should come up with the following data:

Jupiter Diameter ÷ Pluto Diameter = 62.61
Jupiter is nearly 63 times wider than Pluto.

Saturn Diameter ÷ Pluto Diameter = 52.78
Saturn is nearly 53 times wider than Pluto.

Uranus Diameter ÷ Pluto Diameter = 22.38
Uranus is more than 22 times wider than Pluto.

Neptune Diameter ÷ Pluto Diameter = 21.68
Neptune is nearly 22 times wider than Pluto.

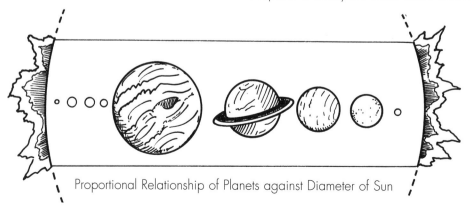

Proportional Relationship of Planets against Diameter of Sun

Mars Diameter ÷ Pluto Diameter = 2.97
Mars is nearly 3 times wider than Pluto.

Earth Diameter ÷ Pluto Diameter = 5.58
Earth is nearly 5.5 times wider than Pluto.

Calculating Inferior Planet Sizes

Continue using Pluto to divide the inferior planets Venus and Mercury for the following results:

Venus Diameter ÷ Pluto Diameter = 5.29
Venus is a little over 5 times wider than Pluto.

Mercury Diameter ÷ Pluto Diameter = 2.13
Mercury is a little over 2 times wider than Pluto.

Calculating the Size of the Sun

The diameter of the Sun is so much larger than the diameter of Pluto that we should substitute Jupiter for Pluto in this final calculation:

Diameter of the Sun ÷ Diameter of Jupiter = 9.72
The Sun is nearly 10 times wider than Jupiter.

Making the Scale Drawing

With these calculations you can begin making your scaled drawing. Find an equivalent unit of measurement to represent Pluto's diameter. Remember, the size differential between Pluto and the Sun is so enormous—the Sun being about 600 times wider than

Pluto—that you'll want as small an equivalent unit of measurement for the diameter of Pluto as possible. Try using ⅛ inch (0.31 cm) to start. Using your diameter comparisons and a calculator, add ⅛-inch (0.31-cm) measurements to determine the diameter of the remaining planets. For example, if Pluto's diameter is ⅛ inch (0.31 cm), then the diameter of Jupiter would be nearly 8 inches (19.37 cm) and the diameter of the Sun about 6 feet 3 inches (1.9 m)! If these sizes seem unwieldy, substitute a smaller measurement for the diameter of Pluto.

For the next step, use the tape measure to find the middle point of each planet's diameter by measuring the diameter and dividing by 2. For the smaller planets Pluto, Mercury, Mars, Venus, and Earth, make a mark at the middle point and place the needle of the compass on the mark. Sweep the compass in a complete circle so that you trace the circumference of each planet. (Pluto and Mercury are so small that with a steady hand you can trace a circle without using the compass.) For the larger planets Neptune, Uranus, Saturn, and Jupiter, find the middle point and mark it. But this time, measure out a length of string from the middle point to the diameter's end and tape it to the mark. Tie a pencil to the end of the string and, holding the string taut, carefully sweep the pencil around in a circle. You will trace out the circumference of the larger planets.

	Diameter (miles)	Diameter (km)
Sun	864,400	1,383,040
Mercury	3,031	4,878
Venus	7,520	12,103
Earth	7,926	12,756
Mars	4,217	6,786
Jupiter	88,846	142,948
Saturn	74,898	120,536
Uranus	31,763	51,118
Neptune	30,775	49,528
Pluto	1,419	2,284

Coloring Your Drawing

To add a realistic touch, you can paint each of your larger planets to simulate their appearance in space. Use accurate scientific illustrations and space-probe photographs as a guide for surface details or cloud formations.

Display Tip

Because the Sun is so large, placing it alongside the other planets of the solar system may result in too large a drawing to display in your booth. Instead, try using the Sun as a background for the rest of the planets.

Measure Atmospheric Reflection, or "Earth Shine"

You Will Need

- 2 large pieces of black poster board
- Black matte paint
- Small paintbrush (*for black matte paint*)
- White paint
- Large paintbrush (*for white paint*)
- Ping-Pong ball
- Wooden skewer stick
- Small Styrofoam block
- Hooded lamp with low-watt bulb
- Black or dark-colored sheet
- Sharp nail
- Masking tape
- Table

"Earth Shine" Setup

When we see the phases of the moon, we usually see only the illuminated portion while the rest of the moon's disc remains hidden. But sometimes the ghost of a full moon remains through its phases. You can sometimes see this beautiful effect during the quarter-moon phase. What is this phenomenon, and why does it happen? This project will help you understand atmospheric reflection, or "Earth shine."

Procedure

1. With the small paintbrush, paint half of the Ping-Pong ball black. Allow the paint to dry.

2. Use the nail to punch a small hole where the black half of the Ping-Pong ball joins the white half. Push one end of the skewer stick through the hole until it touches the top of the Ping-Pong ball. Push the other end of the skewer stick into the Styrofoam block. This is your moon model.

3. Cut, fold, and tape one piece of black poster board so that it supports the other piece of board in an almost vertical position (see illustration). Use the nail to punch a viewing hole in the center of the vertical poster board.

4. Place the poster board on the edge of a table, and position the lamp in front so that the light from the hood falls directly on the lower half of the poster board, but away from the hole you punched. Make sure no part of the lamp blocks your view when you look through the hole.

5. Put the moon model at the opposite edge of the table, and rotate the Ping-Pong ball so that you see a white "quarter moon" when you look through the viewing hole in the poster board.

6. Hang the black sheet behind the moon model.

7. Switch on the lamp, and turn off any other room lights. Look at the quarter moon through the viewing hole in the poster

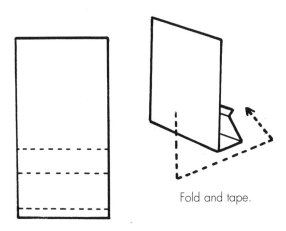

Fold and tape.

Stand Construction

board. Record your observations. Then turn the room lights on and switch off the lamp.

8. With the white paint and large paintbrush, paint cloud formations on the side of the poster board facing the moon model. Make the clouds large and thick so that they turn the black poster board almost completely white.

9. With the lamp positioned as before, turn off the room lights and observe the quarter moon through the viewing hole. Record your observations.

Result

Although for both viewings you will probably see the entire Ping-Pong ball, the first viewing, through the black poster board, revealed a bright white quarter moon with the rest of the moon fairly blending into the blackness of the sheet behind. The second viewing, through the cloud-painted poster board, revealed not only a bright quarter moon, but the rest of the moon's disc standing out from the blackness of the sheet behind. This was a moon illuminated by "Earth shine."

Explanation

The poster board painted white with "clouds" represents an Earth atmosphere of high reflectivity. This kind of atmosphere occurs during times of particularly thick cloud cover. Hurricanes, polar storms, and even certain types of pollution can contribute to a highly reflective Earth atmosphere. So the next time you see the sphere of the moon glowing between its phases, you'll know that the reason for it has to do with our own stormy weather.

Demonstrate the Pulse of Pulsars

<table>
<tr><td>

You Will Need

- 2 D-size batteries (1.5 volts)
- Ping-Pong ball
- Modeling clay
- 2 wooden skewer sticks
- Construction paper
- Electrical tape
- Flashlight bulb and bulb holder
- Wires
- Sharp nail
- Screwdriver
- Revolving platform ("lazy Susan")

</td></tr>
</table>

An exploding star, or *nova*, throws hundreds of millions of tons of gas and debris into space and makes a spectacular show for astronomers. Some novae, like the Horsehead Nebula in the constellation Andromeda, have been around for thousands of years. But not every exploding star completely annihilates itself. Some leave a highly compressed piece of star material behind. This material is so dense that its individual atoms have been stripped of their electrons. The cores of these atoms, called neutrons, pack tightly together to make a *neutron star*. As this project will show, some neutron stars can behave very strangely.

Assembling the Star

Procedure

1. Tape the two batteries together end to end, making sure that the positive side of one battery touches the negative side of the other battery. Wrap a piece of construction paper around the batteries and tape it.

2. Use the nail to punch two small holes on opposite sides of the Ping-Pong ball. Stick a skewer stick into each of the holes.

3. Punch a larger hole in the Ping-Pong ball between the sticks. This hole should be large enough to contain the flashlight bulb.

Pulsar Device

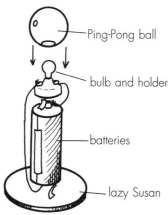

Wrap clay around skewer stick and smooth.

Ping-Pong ball

bulb and holder

batteries

lazy Susan

Wrapping Ping-Pong Ball   Assembly   Operation

4. With the sticks still attached, wrap modeling clay around the Ping-Pong ball, taking care not to cover the hole for the flashlight bulb.

5. Smooth the clay around your pulsar; then remove the skewer sticks.

6. Attach the wires to the terminals of the flashlight-bulb holder, and tape the end of each wire to opposite sides of the batteries.

7. Tape the bulb holder to the top of the battery stack, and carefully place the Ping-Pong ball over the flashlight bulb, fitting the bulb into the hole you made.

8. Put the star device in the center of the revolving platform. Position the star so that it's as close to the center of the platform as possible and doesn't wobble.

9. Dim the lights, place your face at the same level of the ball, and rotate the platform.

Result

Two points of light escape from opposite sides of the star. As you spin the pulsar on its revolving platform, these points of light appear and disappear at regular intervals.

Explanation

Neutron stars spin very rapidly. Some of them appear to have "hot spots" of radiation (in the form of radio signals) on opposite sides that flash or pulse as the neutron star revolves. Neutron stars that behave this way are called *pulsars,* and scientists measure the frequency of radiation pulse to determine both the size of the star and its rate of spin. The points of light on the ball represent flashes of radiation from a pulsar. By timing the interval between each flash, scientists can calculate the rotational speed of pulsars.

Construct a Classic Gnomon Sundial

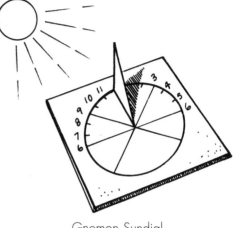

Gnomon Sundial

You Will Need

- 2 large corrugated grocery boxes
- Scissors
- Compass
- Protractor
- Felt-tip marking pen
- Yardstick, meterstick, or straightedge
- Glue
- Masking tape

Human beings probably first learned to mark the time by studying the shift of shadows throughout the day. Archeologists believe that many ancient structures, such as Stonehenge in England and the pyramids of Egypt, were somehow designed to mark the time, seasons, or movements of stars. Ancient Greek astronomers probably designed the familiar garden sundial, which consists of a dial and gnomon (triangular marker).

Although this sundial is easy to construct, you shouldn't convert the Imperial measurements directly into their metric equivalents. Instead, use the Imperial and metric measurements interchangeably. A sundial built in centimeters will be about half as large as one built in inches.

Procedure

1. Cut two 20-inch-square pieces of cardboard from the grocery boxes.

2. Use the yardstick and marking pen to draw lines connecting the opposite corners of one of the squares of cardboard. Where the lines intersect is the center of the cardboard.

3. Adjust the compass so that the needle and pencil ends are 9 inches apart. Place the needle end of the compass in the center of the cardboard and drag the pencil side around to draw a complete circle. Your circle should be 18 inches across.

4. Divide half of the circle into 12 evenly spaced points along the circumference. Starting at the left side, number the points 6, 7, 8, 9, 10, 11, 12, 1, 2, 3, 4, 5.

5. To make the gnomon, take the second piece of cardboard and draw a line 8 inches long. This is the base.

6. For an accurate time reading, the gnomon must have the same angle as the latitude where you live. You can find the latitude of your location by either looking on an atlas or referring to the chart.

7. Use the protractor to mark off the angle at one end of the base.

8. Draw a line 20 inches long from the end of the base through the angle mark. Connect that line to the other end of the base so that you have a narrow triangle. This is your gnomon. Cut it out.

9. Take the base of the gnomon and fold it up about ¼ inch.

10. On the dial, draw a line from the number 12 to the center of the circle and mark a point 1 inch from the center.

11. Apply glue to the underside of the fold, and place the gnomon so that its angle touches the 1-inch mark.

12. Now you must position your sundial so that the gnomon points north. To do this, you can either use a navigator's compass or wait until after dark when you can see the North Star.

12. Set your sundial up in a sunny spot and anchor it so that it can't be easily moved. Check your dial throughout the day.

13. To tell the time with your sundial, look at the shadow the gnomon casts against the dial. Where the edge of the shadow falls indicates the hour of day.

Explanation

As the Sun moves across the sky, the gnomon casts a shadow against the dial. Where the edge of the shadow falls indicates the hour of day. The position of the shadow against the dial provides an accurate reading of solar time—that is, time calculated entirely from the apparent east-to-west motion of the Sun across the sky. Solar time is different from standard time because solar time recognizes no time zones.

Since the Earth is round, when you travel, the ground curves slightly and a different part of the sky appears directly overhead. If your friend, living in a town 20 miles (32 km) west of you, had a sundial identical to yours, he would experience 12 noon a few minutes later than you.

Display Tip

Make a chart comparing standard and solar time throughout the day. Does your dial tell you it's 12 noon before your wristwatch does, or is it the other way around? What can this information tell you about your latitude? How will daylight saving time affect your comparison?

Gnomon Sundial Construction

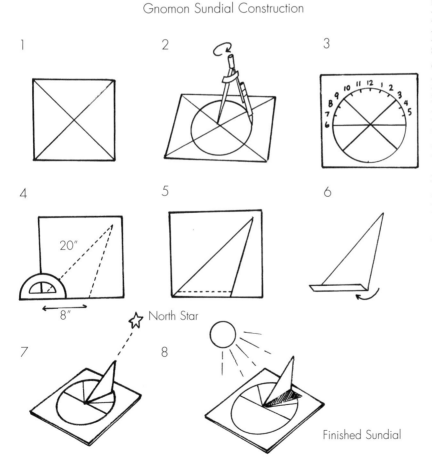

Finished Sundial

Use Solar Radiation to Distill Water

What would happen if your were stuck in the wilderness—hot, thirsty, and without water except for a muddy stream washing by? Of course you could drink the muddy water, but it would probably taste terrible. It might also contain harmful microorganisms. But if you had the materials listed above, you could make all the clean water you wanted.

Procedure

1. Mix some dirt and water together in a bucket. Make sure your muddy water isn't too thick.

2. Pour the muddy water into the washbasin. Make sure the water isn't more than 2 inches deep.

3. Place the basin in a place where it gets good sun all day.

4. Put one of the clean rocks in the drinking glass, and put the glass in the center of the washbasin. If the glass wants to float up in the water, put another rock into it.

5. Cover the top of the basin with the cellophane wrap. Use no more wrap than is necessary, and pull it tightly around the edges of the basin. Tape it to secure it.

6. Put the second rock on the cellophane, directly over the drinking glass. The rock should be heavy enough to stretch the cellophane down toward the glass.

7. Check your distiller throughout the day.

Result

Beads of water form on the underside of the cellophane. They slide down toward the center of the cellophane where they combine and become heavy enough to drop into the drinking glass. After a full day in the sun, your glass should be filled with clear water. This water may not taste so wonderful, but it will be clean and safe to drink.

Explanation

It gets very hot under the cellophane—hot enough to evaporate the muddy water. The water vapor rises and collects in small beads on the underside of the cellophane. These beads are made of pure, *distilled* water—that is, heated water that rises and leaves impurities (like dirt) behind. Because the cellophane sags to the center of the basin, the beads slide down and combine into large drops that fall into the drinking glass.

Display Tip

Time how long it took your solar distiller to collect a full glass of pure water. Try adding more or less dirt to your water. Is the distiller's efficiency affected? Use different liquids, like saltwater, in your distiller and record the result. How would you use the distiller if *no water* had been readily available?

A. Setup

B. Condensation on cellophane falls into cup.

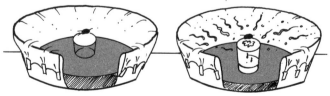

Cutaway View of Basin with Cellophane and Cup

Planetary Surface Illusions

You Will Need

- Large square sheet of red poster board
- Pencil
- String
- Black paint
- Paintbrush
- Black or dark-colored sheet
- Masking tape
- Scissors
- Binoculars
- Large room or space

In 1877 the Italian astronomer Giovanni Schiaparelli thought that he saw something unusual on Mars. His telescope was powerful enough to make out surface features on the Red Planet, but not precise enough to bring those features into sharp focus. The result was that Schiaparelli proclaimed to the world that the surface of Mars was covered with a network of canals. Many people soon believed that Martian engineers built these canals to save their parched and dying planet, a myth that found its ultimate expression in Orson Welles's radio drama of 1933.

With the improvement of telescope design in the 1920s, the first accurate map of the Red Planet was made by the French astronomer Eugene Antoniadi. It cast doubt on the reality of the Martian canals, but the idea of Martian canals has persisted almost to the present day. In fact, only with the launch of the American *Viking* probes has the myth of canals (and the Martians who built them) been completely disproved.

People still claim to see odd things on Mars, however, and even the most detailed photographs show unusual features that many believe indicate intelligent life once existed on the planet. Perhaps the most famous of these is the "giant face" found in the Valles Marineris, or deep canyon region of the planet's equator. But most serious astronomers dismiss these claims for reasons you will explore in this project.

The Elusive Canals of Mars

Procedure

1. Dilute the black paint until it's fairly watery but still opaque. Dip the paintbrush into the paint, stand a few feet (about 1 m) from the red poster board, and spatter the

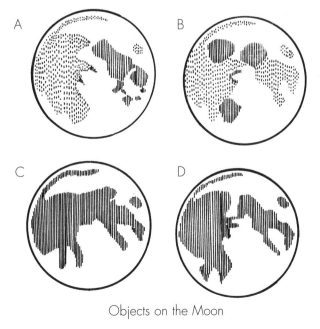

Objects on the Moon

board with small droplets. Keep your spattering spontaneous, but try not to move your brush too quickly, so that the dots clump into several areas on the poster board.

2. After the paint dries, tie one end of a length of string to the pencil. Tape the free end of the string to the center of the red poster board, and twist the pencil until you have a string length a little less than half the width of the poster board. Hold the pencil so that the string is taut, and sweep the pencil around to trace a large circle. Cut out the circle.

3. Use a few safety pins to attach the circle to the center of the dark-colored sheet.

4. Tape the sheet to a wall, and stand about 30 feet (9 m) away. Using only your eyes, observe the shapes on "Mars," and make a sketch of what you see.

5. Twist the focus of the binoculars before you place them against your face. Look at "Mars" through the binoculars, and observe the blurry shapes you see. Do any of these shapes appear the result of conscious design? Refine your sketch if necessary. See how we drew objects on the moon (page 195) for an example.

6. Gradually twist the focus so that your Martian image becomes clearer. Do the shapes persist?

Explanation

The arbitrary arrangement of dots on Mars forms familiar shapes and patterns when your viewing is blurred. To the untrained eye, these shapes might appear the result of deliberate design and intelligent life. This is because the human brain loves to make connections, both spatial and logical. When it comes to astronomy, these abilities have helped organize the complexities of cosmic data. For example, the earliest Babylonian astronomers looked up and saw creatures, people, and marvelous objects in the confusion of stars. Their names for what they saw were passed to the Greeks and then to the Romans, who translated them into Latin. We still use the Latin names today.

Calculate Time from Stellar Motion

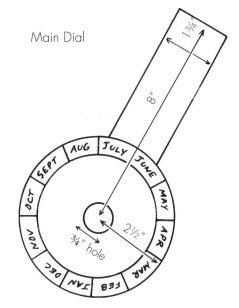

Main Dial

You Will Need

- Thick 2 × 2-foot (60 × 60-cm) poster board or card stock
- Ruler
- Compass
- Protractor
- Felt-tip marking pen
- Thread
- Tape
- Glue
- Scissors
- Flashlight (optional)
- Red cellophane (optional)

The Sun isn't the only astronomical body from which the time can be calculated. As calendars became standardized and more accurate, many devices appeared that could calculate time by means other than the movement of the Sun. Medieval navigators were particularly fond of a nocturnal star clock that used the fixed position of the North Star, or *Polaris,* and concentric calendar wheels to determine the hour. The star clock is really just a simple extension of the analog clockface, applied to the apparent movements of the constellations around a fixed point. This one is accurate, useful, and easy to construct.

Assembling the Star Clock

Procedure

1. Copy the 6 pieces of the star clock onto the poster board in the dimensions indicated.

2. Cut out the largest circular piece. This is the main dial.

3. Using the marking pen and ruler, divide the main dial into 12 pie slices and write the first letter of the month of the year on each pie slice.

4. Cut out the smaller circular piece. This is the time dial.

5. Divide the time dial into 24 pie slices, one slice for each hour of a 24-hour day. Or, you can divide the dial into two 12-hour halves indicating A.M. and P.M.

Note: The protractor can help you divide the circle evenly into 24 sections. Divide the 360 degrees of a circle by 24 for a quotient of 15. Place the protractor over the circle's center, and make hatch marks every 15 degrees. Draw lines connecting each hatch mark with the center of the circle.

6. Cut out all the remaining pieces and assemble the star clock, following the diagram.

7. Cut 2 pieces of thread and tape them across the center hole of the star clock so that they cross each other perpendicularly. These are your crosshairs for sighting Polaris.

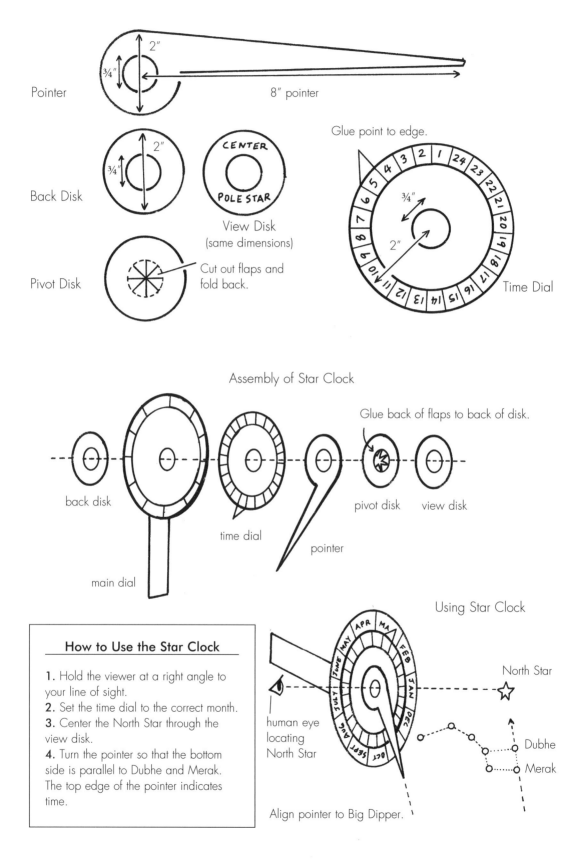

Pointer

2"

¾"

8" pointer

Back Disk

2"

¾"

CENTER

POLE STAR

View Disk
(same dimensions)

Glue point to edge.

¾"

2"

Time Dial

Pivot Disk

Cut out flaps and
fold back.

Assembly of Star Clock

Glue back of flaps to back of disk.

back disk

time dial

pointer

pivot disk   view disk

main dial

Using Star Clock

North Star

Dubhe

Merak

human eye
locating
North Star

Align pointer to Big Dipper.

How to Use the Star Clock

1. Hold the viewer at a right angle to
your line of sight.
2. Set the time dial to the correct month.
3. Center the North Star through the
view disk.
4. Turn the pointer so that the bottom
side is parallel to Dubhe and Merak.
The top edge of the pointer indicates
time.

Using the Star Clock

Procedure

1. Take your clock out on a clear, starry night, preferably one without a full moon.

2. Rotate the time dial so that its pointer indicates the correct month on the main dial.

Note: If you need light for setting up the clock, wrap a flashlight in red cellophane. The light from the flashlight is sufficient for reading but won't ruin your eyes for night viewing.

3. To locate Polaris, first find the Big Dipper. The two stars at the far end of the Dipper—named Merak and Dubhe—point directly to Polaris. Use these "pointer stars" to guide you.

4. Hold the clock flat against your face and look through the center hole of the view disc for Polaris, lining it up in the crosshairs.

5. While keeping your sight on Polaris, carefully move the pointer until it's parallel to the two pointer stars in the Big Dipper (see diagram, page 198, lower right). The straight edge of the pointer will indicate the time on the time dial.

Explanation

In the Northern Hemisphere, Polaris remains a fixed point in the sky around which all the other stars revolve in a counterclockwise direction. This means that you can think of Polaris as the center of a giant clock dial and the stars' motion around it indicating the hour. Since the Big Dipper is one of the most recognizable constellations and conveniently close to Polaris, we chose it as the "hour hand" of our star clock.

If the Earth didn't orbit the Sun as it rotated, then you would find the stars in the same place each night. But because of the Earth's orbit, we look out into space in a slightly different direction every 24 hours. This means that the stars reach the same position 4 minutes earlier each night. The cumulative result of this apparent movement is why the calendar dial is necessary.

At night, a star clock gives you the same local apparent time (based on noon at your local longitude) that a sundial provides during the day. This means that your clock, when measured against a standard timepiece, will be off by several minutes depending on three factors: (1) your longitude, (2) whether you are on daylight saving time, (3) the variation in noon-to-noon time due to the Earth's elliptical orbit and its inclined axis.

Construct a Daytime Moon Locator

You Will Need

- 8-inch (20-cm) square cardboard
- 8½ × 19-inch (21.25 × 47.5-cm) sheet of poster board
- Ruler
- Protractor
- Felt-tip marking pen
- Pencil with eraser
- Scissors
- Tape
- Craft knife
- Compass
- Thumbtack

The Moon's position is a continual surprise for even the most devoted sky watchers. Over the course of a month, the Moon appears at night, during the day, and in various parts of the sky. During the new Moon phase, it's on the opposite side of Earth and doesn't appear at all. This daytime Moon locator combines the lunar calendar, a compass, and a sighting instrument in a simple device that allows you to find the Moon, even when it's invisible.

Assembling the Locator

Procedure

1. Using the pencil and ruler, draw lines connecting opposite corners of the poster board. Place the point of the compass where the lines intersect at the center, and draw a circle on the poster board 8 inches (20 cm) in diameter.

2. Place the protractor over the center, and use the pencil to make hatch marks 12 degrees apart so that you divide the circle into 30 pie-shaped wedges. Cut out this "dial."

3. Draw a smaller circle inside the dial so that you have a rim of boxes at the dial's edge.

4. Erase all pencil lines except for the center point and rim of boxes. Draw over the boxes with the felt-tip marking pen.

5. Moving counterclockwise, number the first box "0", then continue numbering the remaining boxes 1 through 29. These boxes represent the days of the lunar month.

6. Turn the dial so that the numbers always face you and begin filling in the phases of the Moon. In the 0 box, draw a solid circle for the new Moon. In box 7, draw a first quarter half-Moon (the dark half is on the right). In box 15, draw an empty circle for the full Moon. In box 23, draw a last quarter half-Moon (the dark half also on the right).

7. Following the diagram, score the cardboard with the craft knife, and then fold it to make a wedge-shaped stand.

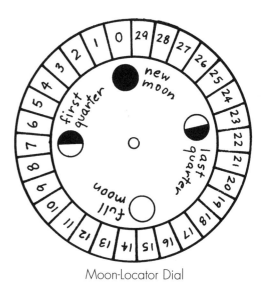

Moon-Locator Dial

8. Angle C of your stand must equal the angle of your latitude. To find your latitude, consult a globe. The lines of latitude (indicating the distance from the Equator) run from east to west so that the Equator is at 0 degrees latitude, and the poles are at 90 degrees. Locate the latitude line closest to your city.

9. Fold the stand again, this time measuring angle C with the protractor. When angle C matches your latitude, tape the stand together, trimming the excess cardboard where necessary.

10. Attach the dial to the stand with a thumbtack. Make sure the dial rotates freely.

Using the Lunar Locator

Procedure

1. Find what day of the lunar month it is by checking a newspaper. Use the pencil to lightly mark the corresponding box of your dial.

2. Take your lunar locator outside and position it so that the low end of the stand faces north.

3. Turn the dial so that box 0 points toward the Sun.

4. You can find the Moon's position by imagining a line going out from the center of the dial, through the marked box, and toward the horizon.

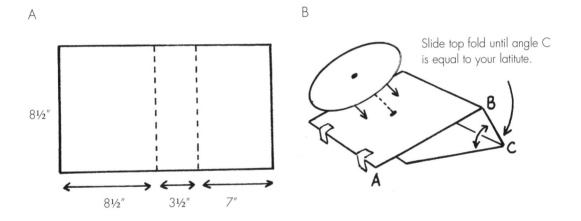

A

8½"

8½" 3½" 7"

B

Slide top fold until angle C is equal to your latitude.

B

C

A

Assembly of Moon Locator

Simulate a Partial & Full Solar Eclipse

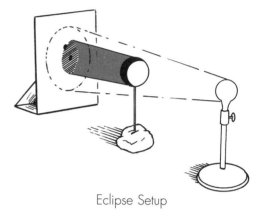

Eclipse Setup

Although the Sun is much larger than our Moon, it's also much farther away. This means that, from the Earth, both the Sun and Moon appear to be the same size. When the Moon's disc crosses in front of the Sun, it can either partially or totally block the Sun's light—a solar eclipse. When the Earth passes directly between the Moon and the Sun, the Moon is thrown into the Earth's shadow—a lunar eclipse.

Eclipses are important because they help scientists observe details of a planet's atmosphere that would ordinarily remain invisible. For example, full solar eclipses give scientists a rare and breathtaking view of the Sun's corona, or mantle of gases. And scientists love to study the Earth's shadow as it passes in front of the Moon because the shadow reveals much about the Earth's atmosphere.

In this project you will build a simple device that simulates a full and partial solar eclipse. Your project will allow you to view the "corona" of your lightbulb Sun.

Procedure

1. Make a Moon from some of the modeling clay and make a base for the Moon out of the remaining clay.

2. Push one end of the skewer stick into the Moon and push the other end into the base. Stand this stick-Moon upright.

3. Remove the shade from a small lamp and place the lamp about 14 inches (35 cm) behind the stick-Moon. The lightbulb should be at the same level as the Moon. You may need to elevate your stick-Moon with a couple of books.

4. Cut, fold, and tape one piece of poster board so that it supports the other piece of board in an almost vertical position.

5. Switch on the lamp so that it throws a circular shadow on the poster board. If the shadow is too big or fuzzy, move the lamp so that you get a clearer shadow, but avoid moving the lamp too close to the Moon.

6. Make three marks on the circular shadow, one directly in the center of the shadow, and two others on the edge of the shadow. Use the sharp nail to punch a hole through each of the marks.

7. On the other side of the poster board, indicate which hole is at the center of the shadow.

8. Dim the room lights, walk behind the poster board, and look through one of the edge holes first. Then look through the center hole.

Result

When you look through each edge hole, you will see a good simulation of a partial solar eclipse. Notice how the light spills out from one side of the Moon's disc while the remainder of the Sun's light is blocked or *occulted.*

When you look through the center hole, you'll see a full solar eclipse simulated. Notice the softer light shooting from the edges of your Moon—an effect that simulates the Sun's corona.

Explanation

When a solar eclipse occurs, the Moon's shadow is thrown across the surface of the Earth. Depending on where you are in that shadow—which is about 155 miles (248 km) wide—you'll see either a full or partial eclipse. Because the Earth rotates, the shadow, or *umbra*, races across the Earth's surface tracing out an "eclipse track."

Compare Standard & Mean Astronomical Time

You Will Need

- World map or globe
- Notebook
- Pencil or pen

For most of us, the time we read on our wristwatches, standard civil time, does not accurately reflect the real time of astronomical events. In fact, a sundial gives us a more accurate reading because it represents *mean astronomical time*, or time measured by the movement of the Sun, Moon, and planets across the sky. As this project will show, mean astronomical time may differ from standard time by many minutes, depending on the observer's location.

Why the Difference?

Since the Earth is round, when you travel the ground curves slightly and a different part of the sky appears directly overhead. When the Sun is at its highest point in one location—*local apparent noon*—it's a minute short of noon a few miles west, and a minute past noon a few miles east.

Odd Times

Only a little over a century ago, cities and towns across America set their clocks slightly differently to reflect these variations. As railway systems developed, confusion resulted from the many different local times used along the lines. The first step toward developing standard time was the introduction of so-called *railway time*—the local civil time of an important rail station. As interstate and international communication expanded with the inventions of the telegraph and telephone, people all over the world saw the need for a universal standard.

The Invention of Standard Time

In 1884 the International Meridian Conference adopted a system of standard time, dividing the Earth's surface into 24 zones. The standard time for each zone is the mean astronomical time of one of 24 meridians (lines of longitude), 15 degrees apart, beginning at Greenwich, England. These meridians extend east and west around the globe to the international dateline.

Standard time is the mean astronomical time at an agreed-upon standard longitude. In the continental United States, for instance, these longitudes are 75 degrees West (eastern time), 90 degrees West (central time), 105 degrees West (mountain time), and 120 degrees West (Pacific time).

Moving east of Greenwich, the city of Rome is 15 degrees East. Cairo is 45 degrees East, and Tokyo is 135 degrees East.

Mean Astronomical-Time Calculations

If you live directly along one of the meridians, standard time and mean astronomical time are the same. But if you live between meridians, you can easily calculate mean astronomical time using only a map, notebook, and pencil to do the simple arithmetic.

Procedure

1. Consult the map to determine how many degrees of longitude you are from your time-zone standard.

2. Multiply this number by 4 to find your correction in minutes. If you're east of standard longitude, your correction is a positive number; if you're west, it's negative.

3. Apply this correction to standard time to get your mean astronomical time. Subtract an hour if daylight saving time (DST) is in effect.

4. For example, Cambridge, Massachusetts, sits at 71 degrees west longitude.

Subtract this from 75 degrees (since eastern standard time applies here) and multiply by 4. The correction is plus 16 minutes. So 12:00 midnight eastern standard time is 12:16 A.M. mean astronomical time. In Cambridge celestial objects rise, cross, and set 16 minutes earlier than they do at the standard longitude.

5. Compare your local mean astronomical time with mean astronomical time at various global locations. Where would you find the greatest difference between the two measurements? Display your result in a table.

INDEX